WELCOME TO LE WITH WORD SEA

Learning a new language can be both challenging and rewarding. This book provides puzzle based vocabulary exercises and is intended to supplement traditional methods of language study. We believe that learning should be fun. If you are doing something that you enjoy, then it will be easy to stick with.

In Learn GREEK with Word Search Puzzles you will find a collection of 130 bilingual word search puzzles that will challenge you with dozens of interesting categories.

This book includes:

- Diverse categories including: Numbers, Colors, The Body, Weather, Professions, Fruits, Vegetables, Verbs, Opposites, and many more!
- Words hidden horizontally, vertically or diagonally in each puzzle
- Easy to read puzzles
- Challenging and fun!
- Puzzle based learning provides unique learning perspective
- 65 jumbled review puzzles to challenge your memory and lock in those translations with reinforcement learning
- Complete solutions provided.

Keep your Mind Active and Engaged

Studies have shown that continuously challenging your brain with puzzles and games or acquiring new skills such as a new language can help to delay symptoms of dementia and Alzheimer's.
Keeping a sharp mind is a great idea for people of any age.

Learn with Word Search Series

Now featuring 38 challenging languages. Check out our other titles!
If you enjoyed this book, please consider leaving an HONEST review.
If you have any suggestions for future languages or books, or find any mistakes, please let us know at learnwithwordsearch@gmail.com

Happy searching!

Greek Alphabet

The Greek alphabet has 24 letters, and is summarized below for reference with the equivalent English transliterations.

Upper Case	Lower Case	Letter Name	English Equivalent
Α	α	Alpha	a
Β	β	Beta	b
Γ	γ	Gamma	g
Δ	δ	Delta	d
Ε	ε	Epsilon	e
Ζ	ζ	Zeta	z
Η	η	Eta	h
Θ	θ	Theta	th
Ι	ι	Iota	i
Κ	κ	Kappa	k
Λ	λ	Lambda	l
Μ	μ	Mu	m
Ν	ν	Nu	n
Ξ	ξ	Xi	x
Ο	ο	Omicron	o
Π	π	Pi	p
Ρ	ρ	Rho	r
Σ	σ	Sigma	s
Τ	τ	Tau	t
Υ	υ	Upsilon	u
Φ	φ	Phi	ph
Χ	χ	Chi	ch
Ψ	ψ	Psi	ps
Ω	ω	Omega	o

LEARN WITH WORD SEARCH PUZZLES NOTES

1. Only words that are capitalized in the word list are hidden inside the puzzle grid. Lower case words in the word list are included for reference, for completion, or for words and phrases that are too large to fit inside the grid.

2. In general, when a word has multiple gender variations, Learn with Word Search Puzzles defaults to the masculine form to maintain formatting.

3. Some words are common between English and the translated form. This often occurs when loan words are incorporated into other languages and common speech. Congratulations, you are are more fluent than you thought. When this occurs the word is hidden inside the grid twice.

4. For books that translate words between two different writing systems (Latin-Cyrillic, Latin-Greek, etc.), both writing systems are used in the grid.

Dedicated to those who occasionally struggle to find the correct words

NUMBERS

Welcome to Learn with Word Search. It's time to count down to your new vocabulary. Here we go. Three. Two. One Find these number translations in the grid below.

Η	Ψ	Ζ	Α	Δ	Η	Ώ	Ρ	W	Λ	Μ	Ε	Η	Τ	Ρ
Ι	Α	Ο	Ί	Β	Ε	Τ	Α	Δ	Ω	Δ	Ε	Κ	Α	Φ
E	I	G	H	T	Δ	K	H	I	E	E	Ξ	I	E	Ю
E	Δ	Y	O	A	O	H	A	K	Φ	Ά	O	N	Я	N
R	T	E	Σ	Σ	E	P	A	T	F	A	F	X	L	I
H	Δ	E	K	A	T	T	A	I	E	O	I	H	B	E
T	B	Θ	O	A	P	C	P	Ю	U	Σ	U	N	Ύ	N
Ά	W	T	Y	I	Π	N	E	R	Д	T	Σ	R	N	T
Δ	R	E	A	T	I	E	T	N	H	O	T	E	T	E
M	N	I	L	N	X	E	N	I	X	W	I	T	P	K
O	E	L	E	V	E	N	R	T	A	H	Ά	N	I	A
W	F	P	Ό	N	E	T	Ω	X	E	Ύ	S	E	A	N
T	B	I	N	E	E	T	F	I	F	T	O	Π	H	E
M	Ю	E	V	E	M	K	E	S	C	G	X	C	Ά	Δ
I	T	X	N	E	V	E	S	Φ	Я	Ξ	O	V	T	N

ONE	ΕΝΑ
TWO	ΔΥΟ
THREE	ΤΡΙΑ
FOUR	ΤΕΣΣΕΡΑ
FIVE	ΠΕΝΤΕ
SIX	ΕΞΙ
SEVEN	ΕΦΤΑ
EIGHT	ΟΧΤΩ
NINE	ΕΝΝΙΑ
TEN	ΔΕΚΑ
ELEVEN	ΕΝΤΕΚΑ
TWELVE	ΔΩΔΕΚΑ
THIRTEEN	ΔΕΚΑΤΡΙΑ
FOURTEEN	ΔΕΚΑΤΕΣΣΕΡΑ
FIFTEEN	ΔΕΚΑΠΕΝΤΕ

MORE NUMBERS

2

A zillion is often used to describe a huge number, but it doesn't actually have a defined value. We won't make you count to a zillion, but below you will find some more numbers to add to your vocabulary.

Y	Y	Ω	X	I	Λ	I	A	T	N	A	P	A	Σ	I	H
M	T	S	T	R	E	N	E	N	H	N	T	A	I	O	O
E	R	E	E	X	T	O	S	D	B	Φ	Γ	Ξ	Γ	E	O
I	O	V	N	W	O	I	T	S	E	O	E	Δ	Ώ	I	Ύ
G	F	E	E	I	X	A	H	A	T	A	O	Y	P	K	Y
H	W	N	E	T	N	D	K	Δ	K	N	R	Y	Ώ	O	A
T	T	T	E	B	E	E	E	E	T	E	M	H	Ψ	Σ	T
Y	N	E	H	R	Δ	K	Δ	A	Δ	M	T	O	H	I	N
K	N	E	D	O	A	O	Y	E	O	E	P	T	L	Ω	H
K	T	N	E	E	U	T	M	T	Ά	Ξ	I	H	M	M	N
I	U	H	N	T	F	S	A	H	Ύ	H	A	Y	I	E	E
H	X	N	I	I	E	K	A	Π	N	N	N	T	L	U	Π
H	I	O	F	R	E	N	Σ	N	E	T	T	X	L	T	Ό
A	T	I	Ό	A	T	G	I	O	D	A	A	I	I	N	O
H	T	Ί	N	X	C	Y	T	N	E	V	E	S	O	M	P
Д	H	E	A	D	A	E	I	G	H	T	E	E	N	Θ	T

SIXTEEN	ΔΕΚΑΕΞΙ
SEVENTEEN	ΔΕΚΑΕΦΤΑ
EIGHTEEN	ΔΕΚΑΟΧΤΩ
NINETEEN	ΔΕΚΑΕΝΝΙΑ
TWENTY	ΕΙΚΟΣΙ
THIRTY	ΤΡΙΑΝΤΑ
FORTY	ΣΑΡΑΝΤΑ
FIFTY	ΠΕΝΗΝΤΑ
SIXTY	ΕΞΗΝΤΑ
SEVENTY	ΕΒΔΟΜΗΝΤΑ
EIGHTY	ΟΓΔΟΝΤΑ
NINETY	ΕΝΕΝΗΝΤΑ
HUNDRED	ΕΚΑΤΟ
THOUSAND	ΧΙΛΙΑ
MILLION	ΕΝΑ ΕΚΑΤΟΜΜΥΡΙΟ

DAYS OF THE WEEK

3

The seven days of the week were named after the seven celestial bodies that were visible to the naked eye thousands of years ago. These are the Sun, Moon, Mercury, Venus, Mars, Jupiter, and Saturn. See if you can spot their translations with your naked eye below.

N	T	T	B	Y	H	K	A	I	P	Y	K	A	Σ	Δ
S	A	T	U	R	D	A	Y	I	N	Π	U	A	T	E
X	Ά	T	W	E	E	K	O	T	A	B	B	A	Σ	Y
I	T	O	I	T	S	Ψ	A	P	L	B	D	Y	Σ	T
Y	O	A	A	O	A	D	A	N	A	B	A	H	E	E
T	E	D	I	Ύ	N	Σ	A	T	N	D	Y	T	Θ	P
T	T	S	X	Γ	K	A	O	Y	S	Σ	A	Π	X	A
H	O	C	T	E	P	K	L	E	A	P	K	M	T	K
M	D	M	Y	E	Y	A	N	H	T	D	F	E	H	Ξ
E	A	H	O	P	R	D	H	H	O	X	N	Π	U	F
P	Y	T	I	R	E	D	N	K	T	L	O	U	R	R
A	X	A	A	W	R	O	A	Π	I	I	I	K	S	I
E	K	Y	A	D	N	O	M	Y	P	N	P	D	D	D
O	D	N	E	K	E	E	W	Y	H	Ό	Θ	T	A	A
Σ	H	M	E	P	A	Δ	A	M	O	Δ	B	E	Y	Y

MONDAY	ΔΕΥΤΕΡΑ
TUESDAY	ΤΡΙΤΗ
WEDNESDAY	ΤΕΤΑΡΤΗ
THURSDAY	ΠΕΜΠΤΗ
FRIDAY	ΠΑΡΑΣΚΕΥΗ
SATURDAY	ΣΑΒΒΑΤΟ
SUNDAY	ΚΥΡΙΑΚΗ
WEEKEND	ΣΑΒΒΑΤΟΚΥΡΙΑΚΟ
NATIONAL HOLIDAY	ΕΘΝΙΚΗ ΑΡΓΙΑ
TODAY	ΣΗΜΕΡΑ
TOMORROW	ΑΥΡΙΟ
YESTERDAY	ΧΘΕΣ
WEEK	ΕΒΔΟΜΑΔΑ
DAY	ΗΜΕΡΑ

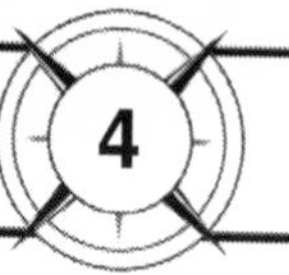

MONTHS

The Roman calendar originally had ten months, which explains why September, October, November and December are based on the latin words for seven, eight, nine and ten. Search for the months and their translations below.

M	J	J	J	T	E	S	N	N	H	E	U	Σ	Σ	Σ	B
O	N	U	A	H	H	H	Y	O	Σ	Σ	E	X	O	K	A
N	O	L	N	D	M	R	I	O	E	Π	H	I	I	E	U
T	V	Y	U	E	A	E	I	A	T	M	P	Ό	N	B	G
H	E	Я	A	U	Φ	P	P	E	N	B	B	Z	Y	Σ	U
Ώ	M	T	R	Σ	B	E	M	O	Ω	Ό	A	P	O	A	S
R	B	B	Y	M	O	B	B	T	Λ	A	H	I	I	E	T
I	E	A	E	E	P	I	K	P	O	O	Λ	A	P	O	Ю
F	R	K	Y	I	A	O	P	O	O	Y	Γ	T	X	M	Σ
H	E	A	O	Γ	E	R	C	A	O	Y	E	I	H	A	O
Δ	C	Σ	M	Я	O	T	E	I	Y	M	A	N	O	P	N
L	I	R	P	A	O	Y	I	Λ	B	O	A	P	O	T	O
Ί	I	B	A	B	Y	C	Σ	E	R	Σ	N	R	I	I	P
D	E	C	E	M	B	E	R	T	Ι	Σ	K	A	Σ	O	X
T	A	R	A	Π	P	I	Λ	I	O	Σ	Δ	Ξ	I	Σ	Σ
N	C	A	L	E	N	D	A	R	A	Σ	O	I	A	M	Q

JANUARY	ΙΑΝΟΥΑΡΙΟΣ
FEBRUARY	ΦΕΒΡΟΥΑΡΙΟΣ
MARCH	ΜΑΡΤΙΟΣ
APRIL	ΑΠΡΙΛΙΟΣ
MAY	ΜΑΙΟΣ
JUNE	ΙΟΥΝΙΟΣ
JULY	ΙΟΥΛΙΟΣ
AUGUST	ΑΥΓΟΥΣΤΟΣ
SEPTEMBER	ΣΕΠΤΕΜΒΡΙΟΣ
OCTOBER	ΟΚΤΩΒΡΙΟΣ
NOVEMBER	ΝΟΕΜΒΡΙΟΣ
DECEMBER	ΔΕΚΕΜΒΡΙΟΣ
CALENDAR	ΗΜΕΡΟΛΟΓΙΟ
MONTH	ΜΗΝΑΣ
YEAR	ΧΡΟΝΟΣ

TIME & SEASONS

5

The seasons are caused by the tilt of the Earth as it orbits the sun. For part of the year the sun shines longer on one hemisphere resulting in summer. Tilt your head and search for these words related to time and the seasons below.

A	D	Π	Д	Я	C	A	F	T	E	R	N	O	O	N
H	W	D	N	O	C	E	S	G	H	E	M	E	A	M
Θ	Ό	O	Π	M	O	R	N	I	N	G	W	Θ	Δ	Ψ
N	Φ	H	P	G	W	I	N	T	E	R	I	W	E	A
T	H	Θ	Ω	N	R	B	A	U	U	Φ	B	N	Y	N
N	X	X	I	P	D	A	Y	E	A	R	T	D	T	O
O	Y	P	S	N	Ύ	T	Δ	E	E	H	Y	Λ	E	I
O	X	X	O	A	O	E	N	M	U	T	U	A	P	Ξ
Σ	T	E	T	N	K	Π	M	O	N	T	H	I	O	H
A	A	Π	I	A	O	U	Ω	I	Д	T	A	E	Λ	M
N	P	N	E	M	S	Σ	Δ	P	N	K	R	D	E	E
Ω	Ω	T	H	Λ	Ω	D	Φ	M	O	U	T	A	Π	P
I	I	E	P	M	S	N	E	Λ	O	F	T	C	T	A
A	Π	O	Γ	E	Y	M	A	H	A	H	H	E	O	A
O	I	O	A	A	Ю	K	T	Σ	P	H	B	D	I	W

WINTER	ΧΕΙΜΩΝΑΣ
SPRING	ΑΝΟΙΞΗ
SUMMER	ΚΑΛΟΚΑΙΡΙ
AUTUMN	ΦΘΙΝΟΠΩΡΟ
SECOND	ΔΕΥΤΕΡΟΛΕΠΤΟ
MINUTE	ΛΕΠΤΟ
HOUR	ΩΡΑ
DAY	ΗΜΕΡΑ
MONTH	ΜΗΝΑΣ
YEAR	ΧΡΟΝΟΣ
MORNING	ΠΡΩΙ
AFTERNOON	ΑΠΟΓΕΥΜΑ
NIGHT	ΝΥΧΤΑ
DECADE	ΔΕΚΑΕΤΙΑ
CENTURY	ΑΙΩΝΑΣ

COLORS

6

The three primary colors are red, green and blue. These three colors can be combined to create an astonishing variety of color. Astonish yourself by finding these translations in the grid below.

E P D M I U Π Ξ Y Ξ K G R E Y

P L O O E G A Я V N R O O Φ Λ

T C M A Λ W H I T E R R I Я M

Λ Z O P Π M A G E N T A Z A A

R Φ N N M O O N A W Я N A Σ X

H Γ I Γ I L P Y N O I G Λ Ύ L

A H K O D P C T N R M E A E Ό

T P K N K E T A O B H Ω Γ Θ M

I I O I H C R I C K Σ T B D Ψ

O I K Σ K R A E K B A H M Y Y

I Ί A A Y E L L O W I Λ M A I

E G Φ P Ί P U K B P Ξ A I Σ Д

N E G Π R E V L I S Y D F Π Π

A Ά A U Y Δ O N B P O Σ Y P X

O A P F H O K Ξ O M Φ F A O I

BLACK
BLUE
BROWN
CYAN
GOLD
GREY
GREEN
MAGENTA
ORANGE
PINK
PURPLE
RED
SILVER
WHITE
YELLOW

ΜΑΥΡΟ
ΜΠΛΕ
ΚΑΦΕ
ΓΑΛΑΖΙΟ
ΧΡΥΣΟ
ΓΚΡΙ
ΠΡΑΣΙΝΟ
ΦΟΥΞΙΑ
ΠΟΡΤΟΚΑΛΙ
ΡΟΖ
ΜΩΒ
ΚΟΚΚΙΝΟ
ΑΣΗΜΙ
ΑΣΠΡΟ
ΚΙΤΡΙΝΟ

SHAPES

A dodecagon has 12 sides, while a megagon has a million sides, at which point it is essentially a circle. Time to think outside the box and find these 2D and 3D shapes in the puzzle below.

W	S	O	N	Ω	Γ	A	T	N	E	Π	Δ	S	Σ	H
K	Λ	H	N	K	K	Y	Λ	I	N	Δ	P	O	Σ	Σ
A	Y	A	C	Ω	A	Σ	T	E	P	I	Λ	T	O	I
D	X	B	B	N	Γ	Ό	Ξ	P	Π	K	N	B	N	O
I	N	E	O	O	B	A	E	Y	Y	Σ	M	Ξ	N	P
M	R	O	J	Σ	Γ	N	P	K	T	O	N	Ω	E	Θ
A	E	T	M	Ω	T	A	T	T	P	I	Γ	Ω	N	O
R	C	Δ	N	A	M	R	C	B	E	A	H	A	B	Γ
Y	T	O	G	I	I	Y	I	O	T	T	S	A	O	Ω
P	A	O	Δ	A	L	D	O	K	N	H	A	C	M	N
C	N	A	N	I	U	A	O	H	Ώ	E	T	I	E	I
U	G	G	N	O	G	A	X	E	H	A	Д	R	S	O
B	L	D	A	P	I	A	Φ	Σ	G	T	P	C	T	A
E	E	R	A	U	Q	S	Γ	O	O	V	A	L	A	F
R	B	T	W	N	Ώ	T	N	P	S	P	H	E	R	E

CIRCLE	ΚΥΚΛΟΣ
CONE	ΚΩΝΟΣ
CUBE	ΚΥΒΟΣ
CYLINDER	ΚΥΛΙΝΔΡΟΣ
DIAMOND	ΡΟΜΒΟΣ
HEXAGON	ΕΞΑΓΩΝΟ
OCTAGON	ΟΚΤΑΓΩΝΟ
OVAL	ΟΒΑΛ
PENTAGON	ΠΕΝΤΑΓΩΝΟ
PYRAMID	ΠΥΡΑΜΙΔΑ
RECTANGLE	ΟΡΘΟΓΩΝΙΟ
SPHERE	ΣΦΑΙΡΑ
SQUARE	ΤΕΤΡΑΓΩΝΟ
STAR	ΑΣΤΕΡΙ
TRIANGLE	ΤΡΙΓΩΝΟ

THE HEAD

Our face is the most expressive part of our body. We can convey a variety of emotions with the 43 muscles we have in our face. Below are some words related to your face and head.

R I E Y E S O N Λ A Ψ A R S E
G I Y C G Σ O Y T E E T H Θ N
O A A D M A Λ Λ I A H B T S R
Φ F J H E H T M T O N G U E Ί
A O T E T A P A Φ E Λ B O H K
K R E Y Ω O C Γ N T Π B M S T
J E M Δ Π H Γ O Y N I Y P A Ύ
S H E H O Λ D Y Π M W I A L N
A E E H Ω N P Λ I Ω L E I E H
N A B Σ C Δ T O T I Σ H Δ Y A
D D Σ T H Θ S I Y X Λ O Y E E
S A L O I N C T A I Ю A P P G
I T A M N E X E E L E K Φ Π E
A Ξ O A T Δ P X A A E O Γ E F
Z E S E E Y E B R O W S S J K

CHEEK	ΜΑΓΟΥΛΟ
CHIN	ΠΗΓΟΥΝΙ
EAR	ΑΥΤΙ
EYE	ΜΑΤΙ
EYEBROWS	ΦΡΥΔΙΑ
EYELASHES	ΒΛΕΦΑΡΑ
FACE	ΠΡΟΣΩΠΟ
FOREHEAD	ΜΕΤΩΠΟ
HAIR	ΜΑΛΛΙΑ
HEAD	ΚΕΦΑΛΙ
LIPS	ΧΕΙΛΗ
MOUTH	ΣΤΟΜΑ
NOSE	ΜΥΤΗ
TEETH	ΔΟΝΤΙΑ
TONGUE	ΓΛΩΣΣΑ

THE BODY

9

The human body is a remarkable thing, with hundreds of specialized parts that we take for granted every day. Here is a list of some important parts of the body to remember.

Θ	Δ	Υ	Ο	Ι	Ρ	Ε	Χ	Ο	Λ	Υ	Τ	Χ	Α	Δ
Η	Α	Α	F	Ε	Α	Ν	Τ	Ι	Χ	Ε	Ι	Ρ	Α	Σ
Λ	Χ	Σ	Α	C	Γ	Ξ	Η	U	Ν	Ε	Ρ	Μ	Σ	Ό
Η	Τ	Α	Λ	Π	Ο	Μ	Ω	Ω	Ύ	Υ	Ε	Ί	Υ	W
Ε	Υ	Ν	Ι	Χ	Φ	Ε	Μ	Ε	Ε	Σ	Χ	Q	Ο	C
Ι	Λ	Ω	Κ	Ψ	Ο	Ο	Τ	Ο	Η	Α	Ν	Κ	Τ	Θ
Ε	Ο	Κ	Α	Ν	Σ	Ώ	Τ	S	Τ	Ε	Χ	Я	Α	Ε
Σ	Π	Γ	Ά	Ν	D	Ο	Ο	Η	Ι	S	Β	Д	Π	Λ
Ε	Ο	Α	Ε	Ο	Ο	Q	Ν	Ο	U	R	Ι	Υ	Ο	J
Ν	Δ	Π	Λ	F	Η	Ν	Ι	U	F	Μ	W	Α	Η	Ψ
Ο	Ι	D	Ρ	Α	Ν	Ι	Ρ	L	Ε	Ι	Β	Α	W	Β
Π	Ο	Δ	Ι	Α	Μ	Ά	Ρ	D	Η	C	Ν	Ο	Ι	Χ
Ι	Υ	Ο	Ρ	L	Κ	Η	L	Ε	Α	D	Β	G	Ε	L
Β	S	Η	Ο	U	L	D	Ε	R	Β	L	Α	D	Ε	Λ
Δ	L	Δ	Ε	L	S	F	Μ	Ω	Ε	Ά	Τ	Κ	L	R

ARM	ΧΕΡΙ
ELBOW	ΑΓΚΩΝΑΣ
FINGER	ΔΑΧΤΥΛΟ ΧΕΡΙΟΥ
FOOT	ΠΑΤΟΥΣΑ
HAND	ΠΑΛΑΜΗ
HIP	ΓΟΦΟΣ
LEG	ΠΟΔΙ
NIPPLE	ΘΗΛΗ
SHOULDER	ΩΜΟΣ
SHOULDER BLADE	ΩΜΟΠΛΑΤΗ
THUMB	ΑΝΤΙΧΕΙΡΑΣ
TOE	ΔΑΧΤΥΛΟ ΠΟΔΙΟΥ
WAIST	ΜΕΣΗ
WRIST	ΚΑΡΠΟΣ

THE BODY 2

10

Skin is the largest human organ and is approximately 15% of your body weight. Search for these other parts of the body and their translations in the puzzle grid below.

C	P	Д	E	H	K	E	W	L	Ω	Ξ	S	O	O	Ψ
Γ	E	B	N	Ω	O	E	E	T	S	K	I	N	Y	H
C	A	F	K	H	Ю	V	Δ	A	C	C	U	D	A	K
U	A	M	I	S	A	O	B	O	I	A	O	M	C	S
Ί	Σ	I	Π	N	T	Γ	T	R	O	B	R	E	A	Ξ
N	T	A	Θ	A	G	T	I	H	E	A	N	K	L	E
P	P	T	N	Σ	U	E	K	T	E	A	M	I	F	N
Σ	A	O	I	B	I	A	R	R	N	R	S	E	Σ	F
O	Γ	P	O	S	T	Π	O	N	K	M	E	T	O	M
P	A	M	P	E	Δ	F	O	Д	A	P	A	H	Θ	Π
H	Λ	A	X	Σ	A	M	M	H	G	I	H	T	H	H
M	O	M	Φ	A	Λ	O	Σ	N	E	T	L	T	T	X
E	Σ	O	M	I	A	Λ	A	P	Y	Γ	Γ	A	Σ	H
O	S	Ω	M	P	E	S	N	Φ	P	X	Λ	L	T	Σ
Y	Σ	Φ	A	T	Y	Ю	A	I	Ά	Π	I	B	B	Σ

ANKLE
ARMPIT
BACK
BODY
BREAST
BUTTOCKS
CALF
FINGERNAIL
FOREARM
KNEE
NAVEL
NECK
SKIN
THIGH
THROAT

ΑΣΤΡΑΓΑΛΟΣ
ΜΑΣΧΑΛΗ
ΠΛΑΤΗ
ΣΩΜΑ
ΣΤΗΘΟΣ
ΟΠΙΣΘΙΑ
ΓΑΜΠΑ
ΝΥΧΙ
ΠΗΧΗΣ
ΓΟΝΑΤΟ
ΟΜΦΑΛΟΣ
ΛΑΙΜΟΣ
ΔΕΡΜΑ
ΜΗΡΟΣ
ΛΑΡΥΓΓΑΣ

ON THE INSIDE

Our internal organs regulate the body's critical systems, providing us with oxygen and energy, and filtering out toxins. Check out this list of squishy but important body parts.

A Y E N D I K N S S G N U L Z Ώ
Ψ I E N I I K M P A N C R E A S
K T N N I A R B U O H C O I M T
A Ω A A Σ T C T V S S K Φ A A O
P K Ξ M Z H S X I T C Λ L Λ T M
Δ Y A H I Ά Δ E S K E L E A Π A
I Σ T O M A X I T B I Π E A E C
A P T H P I E Σ E N T X N S T H
N X A S Π E L Σ T O I Γ N A Θ E
H N R P E I T E E D K E Ξ D E A
Λ E T L V E S N N P O H G Ω E R
Π Φ E E V T T E E I O O Λ R P T
Σ P R E I E P A M Y E Σ L Ω A Θ
Ψ O I N P P Σ I A N X E O B K L
E N E O A Φ E Γ K E Φ A Λ O Σ Σ
S O S S Σ E N O M Y E N Π C O G

APPENDIX	ΣΚΩΛΗΚΟΕΙΔΗΣ αποφυση
ARTERIES	ΑΡΤΗΡΙΕΣ
BLOOD	ΑΙΜΑ
BRAIN	ΕΓΚΕΦΑΛΟΣ
HEART	ΚΑΡΔΙΑ
KIDNEY	ΝΕΦΡΟ
LARGE INTESTINE	ΠΑΧΥ ΕΝΤΕΡΟ
LIVER	ΣΥΚΩΤΙ
LUNGS	ΠΝΕΥΜΟΝΕΣ
MUSCLES	ΜΥΕΣ
PANCREAS	ΠΑΝΓΚΡΕΑΣ
SMALL INTESTINE	ΛΕΠΤΟ ΕΝΤΕΡΟ
SPLEEN	ΣΠΛΗΝΑ
STOMACH	ΣΤΟΜΑΧΙ
VEINS	ΦΛΕΒΕΣ

EARTH

The Earth is an enormous place that time has divided up into continents and oceans. Take some time and memorize these words that define our Earth.

Β Γ N O R T H P O L E H W L A O Γ
Γ Ε Ω Γ Ρ Α Φ Ι Κ Ο Μ Η Κ Ο Σ Μ Ε
H K I P E M A A I E P O B E I X Ω
Κ Β Ο Ρ Ε Ι Ο Σ Π Ο Λ Ο Σ Ρ Α Β Ρ
I N P D H E B Π E Σ S O E O B S Γ
P O H A Ψ N A A O D Λ Σ A R O O A
E R K T C H I P I O U C K U O U Φ
M T I L N I I K Π S I T T E C T I
A H T M O E F Σ O T A H I O T H K
A A K H Π N O I C Σ A F N T H P O
I M P H Π I G R C M Ω T R K A O Π
T E A Д T Ω A I E O I K I I E L Λ
O R T O A T P R T N C P E E C E A
N I N M N Φ I Y E U Φ E Y A N A T
Γ C A A P C T N E A D A A N N N O
N A T L A N T I C O C E A N B O Σ
A T Λ A N T I K O Σ Ω K E A N O Σ

AFRICA	ΑΦΡΙΚΗ
ANTARCTICA	ΑΝΤΑΡΚΤΙΚΗ
ASIA	ΑΣΙΑ
ATLANTIC OCEAN	ΑΤΛΑΝΤΙΚΟΣ ΩΚΕΑΝΟΣ
CONTINENT	ΗΠΕΙΡΟΣ
EUROPE	ΕΥΡΩΠΗ
LATITUDE	ΓΕΩΡΓΑΦΙΚΟ ΠΛΑΤΟΣ
LONGITUDE	ΓΕΩΓΡΑΦΙΚΟ ΜΗΚΟΣ
NORTH AMERICA	ΒΟΡΕΙΑ ΑΜΕΡΙΚΗ
NORTH POLE	ΒΟΡΕΙΟΣ ΠΟΛΟΣ
PACIFIC OCEAN	ΕΙΡΗΝΙΚΟΣ ΩΚΕΑΝΟΣ
SOUTH AMERICA	ΝΟΤΙΑ ΑΜΕΡΙΚΗ
SOUTH POLE	ΝΟΤΙΟΣ ΠΟΛΟΣ

GEOGRAPHY

Time to zoom in and take a look at some geographical features that make up our planet. Fly over mountains, forests and glaciers as you reflect on the beauty of nature.

H	E	W	Y	B	H	B	A	P	S	E	T	Π	N	Ψ
Π	W	X	M	B	Λ	Δ	A	Σ	O	Σ	Σ	A	Γ	Θ
O	I	E	T	Σ	I	A	Φ	H	O	O	Σ	Ί	Σ	X
T	Φ	R	N	E	M	B	Π	N	M	Σ	E	H	Γ	I
A	C	N	X	Σ	N	L	A	H	A	Y	N	K	N	L
M	O	Ώ	F	A	H	E	P	Λ	Λ	E	T	B	A	R
I	R	H	P	N	K	E	A	T	Γ	O	Φ	I	E	L
Σ	A	C	G	Ω	X	Θ	Λ	O	S	V	Π	V	C	M
H	L	A	H	T	K	A	I	C	E	E	I	E	O	A
N	R	E	O	E	Π	Λ	A	N	R	R	R	U	W	C
T	E	B	Γ	Γ	Λ	V	O	L	C	A	N	O	Z	O
D	E	K	P	A	T	H	P	A	Σ	T	T	H	F	A
H	F	I	P	Π	R	E	I	C	A	L	G	E	E	S
N	B	O	Y	N	O	W	S	I	D	E	S	E	R	T
Я	K	Ί	I	S	L	A	N	D	D	T	S	Λ	Ώ	O

BEACH	ΠΑΡΑΛΙΑ
CITY	ΠΟΛΗ
COAST	ΑΚΤΗ
CORAL REEF	ΚΟΡΑΛΛΙΟΓΕΝΗΣ υφαλοσ
CRATER	ΚΡΑΤΗΡΑΣ
DESERT	ΕΡΗΜΟΣ
FOREST	ΔΑΣΟΣ
GLACIER	ΠΑΓΕΤΩΝΑΣ
ISLAND	ΝΗΣΙ
LAKE	ΛΙΜΝΗ
MOUNTAIN	ΒΟΥΝΟ
OCEAN	ΩΚΕΑΝΟΣ
RIVER	ΠΟΤΑΜΙ
SEA	ΘΑΛΑΣΣΑ
VOLCANO	ΗΦΑΙΣΤΕΙΟ

WEATHER

Today's weather forecast shows a 100% chance of learning some important weather terms.

Y	H	Σ	Y	N	N	E	Φ	I	A	Σ	M	E	N	O	Σ
E	Σ	T	L	G	M	S	W	A	R	M	E	I	A	Ξ	H
D	E	O	Σ	A	N	Y	U	A	E	Y	A	T	H	O	T
T	I	H	Y	E	Γ	I	I	N	D	N	N	X	D	T	Σ
Y	Π	A	F	P	Z	N	N	N	N	A	E	Ί	Ξ	O	E
Φ	H	A	A	F	K	Ύ	I	T	U	Y	M	P	T	I	Z
Ω	K	Σ	S	N	O	W	Λ	Σ	H	I	O	Σ	R	N	T
N	I	T	N	P	T	G	P	O	T	G	Y	A	I	A	Ά
A	P	P	L	Γ	Y	Θ	X	Ω	Π	O	I	Ψ	N	P	Я
Σ	T	A	A	H	B	D	D	Ά	Λ	N	M	L	O	Y	I
Ю	E	Π	H	H	Γ	H	U	O	B	I	T	I	I	O	K
H	M	H	X	Ю	T	A	I	O	P	A	T	A	X	M	A
N	O	O	M	N	O	Λ	W	Ξ	L	I	C	Q	B	Λ	Ύ
K	P	Ά	O	R	H	T	U	L	A	C	Ψ	D	H	Ί	H
B	A	P	B	A	R	O	M	E	T	R	I	C	O	L	D
Ψ	B	D	I	M	U	H	U	R	R	I	C	A	N	E	Z

BAROMETRIC pressure	ΒΑΡΟΜΕΤΡΙΚΗ ΠΙΕΣΗ
CLOUDY	ΣΥΝΝΕΦΙΑΣΜΕΝΟΣ
COLD	ΚΡΥΟ
FOG	ΟΜΙΧΛΗ
HOT	ΠΟΛΎ ΖΕΣΤΗ
HUMID	ΥΓΡΑΣΙΑ
HURRICANE	ΤΥΦΩΝΑΣ
LIGHTNING	ΑΣΤΡΑΠΗ
RAIN	ΒΡΟΧΗ
RAINBOW	ΟΥΡΑΝΙΟ ΤΟΞΟ
SNOW	ΧΙΟΝΙ
SUNNY	ΗΛΙΟΛΟΥΣΤΟΣ
THUNDER	ΒΡΟΝΤΗ
WARM	ΖΕΣΤΗ
WINDY	ΜΕ ΑΝΕΜΟ

AFRICAN ANIMALS

15

Let's go on a word safari to search for some of Africa's most famous animals. Elephants and lions are hiding somewhere below.

B	I	O	U	O	M	Ύ	Q	G	I	R	A	F	F	E	E	O
Η	Λ	Α	Δ	Ρ	Α	Π	Ο	Λ	Η	Μ	Α	Κ	Θ	Ρ	W	S
C	T	C	X	I	Μ	Π	Α	Ν	Τ	Ζ	Η	Σ	L	A	B	T
S	A	H	K	E	A	T	E	M	N	O	O	B	A	B	P	R
O	U	I	A	H	L	Λ	Ε	Ο	Π	Α	Ρ	Δ	Α	Λ	Η	I
R	D	M	I	T	N	E	K	I	P	O	C	Δ	B	Σ	E	C
E	G	P	A	Π	E	T	P	I	P	Φ	Υ	Σ	Υ	Λ	Υ	H
C	O	A	Q	T	Π	E	N	H	Θ	A	Φ	I	E	H	Ξ	Y
O	H	N	N	M	O	O	H	Ί	A	A	T	Φ	N	Π	H	E
N	T	Z	D	T	K	P	Π	C	K	N	A	N	A	O	S	N
I	R	E	K	E	E	X	O	O	D	N	T	N	O	Λ	Σ	A
H	A	E	P	Ί	A	L	X	P	T	R	I	B	O	I	A	L
R	W	O	Д	T	Z	O	O	A	P	A	A	M	X	T	Λ	L
T	Σ	H	I	E	I	Ώ	Σ	P	Y	I	M	P	Ό	N	N	I
T	O	Σ	B	P	Θ	A	R	B	E	Z	H	O	O	A	O	R
Σ	T	P	O	Y	Θ	O	K	A	M	H	Λ	O	Σ	E	I	O
Ω	A	Σ	A	Λ	Λ	I	P	O	Γ	P	A	Δ	L	H	L	G

ANTELOPE	ΑΝΤΙΛΟΠΗ
BABOON	ΜΠΑΜΠΟΥΙΝΟΣ
CHEETAH	ΤΣΙΤΑΧ
CHIMPANZEE	ΧΙΜΠΑΝΤΖΗΣ
ELEPHANT	ΕΛΕΦΑΝΤΑΣ
GIRAFFE	ΚΑΜΗΛΟΠΑΡΔΑΛΗ
GORILLA	ΓΟΡΙΛΛΑΣ
HIPPOPOTAMUS	ΙΠΠΟΠΟΤΑΜΟΣ
HYENA	ΥΑΙΝΑ
LEOPARD	ΛΕΟΠΑΡΔΑΛΗ
LION	ΛΙΟΝΤΑΡΙ
OSTRICH	ΣΤΡΟΥΘΟΚΑΜΗΛΟΣ
RHINOCEROS	ΡΙΝΟΚΕΡΟΣ
WARTHOG	ΦΑΚΟΧΟΙΡΟΣ
ZEBRA	ΖΕΒΡΑ

ANIMAL KINGDOM 1

16

A recent study estimated that there are approximately 8.7 million different species of life on Earth. Below are just a few examples for you to learn.

```
Д N Ό K N O O R A G N A K D E
Λ Y K O Σ Ψ U T I I A T Ψ M Σ
A X C A T A Д A U Λ Π I Λ M O
D T H A O J Λ G K M O Γ I P N
A E A B M E N H O Λ N P B E I
H P Ω Γ Π E Д Λ M N T H Я I Y
A I Y O P Z L A A A I Σ Z P O
H Δ Y N H R O P Y O K Γ N A K
P A Y O K Γ A Z T Y I T J Λ Γ
Ψ M D W Σ O Γ A Λ H I A E Y N
X U O B M H H O E G G P T O I
O L G O H T Σ Ό E U E A Ύ M Π
F E U P S C Σ R A B B I T N O
O S O R A E B R A L O P C K I
E M A Δ Y O K P A H K I Λ O Π
```

BAT	ΝΥΧΤΕΡΙΔΑ
CAMEL	ΚΑΜΗΛΑ
CAT	ΓΑΤΑ
DOG	ΣΚΥΛΟΣ
FOX	ΑΛΕΠΟΥ
JAGUAR	ΤΖΑΓΚΟΥΑΡ
KANGAROO	ΚΑΝΓΚΟΥΡΟ
MOOSE	ΑΛΚΗ
MOUSE	ΠΟΝΤΙΚΙ
MULE	ΜΟΥΛΑΡΙ
PENGUIN	ΠΙΝΓΚΟΥΙΝΟΣ
POLAR BEAR	ΠΟΛΙΚΗ ΑΡΚΟΥΔΑ
RABBIT	ΛΑΓΟΣ
TIGER	ΤΙΓΡΗΣ
WOLF	ΛΥΚΟΣ

ANIMAL KINGDOM 2

Another study estimates that approximatley 150-200 species are going extinct every 24 hours. Find the animals below before they disappear forever.

G O M N I K S K C H I P M U N K
N K R A Y Ί P C R O C O D I L E
O S N A Y O Π O Σ O Y M M T W E
O Q Σ U N P K O K I Ί I A X O O
C U F O K G H A Q O K T K M Y Π
C I M S P S U A P A Δ O O P A Σ
A R U K Я I Σ T P L Y E A Λ K Λ
R R S A A N O Y A K Δ K I I K I
A E S G D Σ O X O N O Ά O Λ Σ Γ
E L O O O I T Y O T N Y N I O Π
B L P O K R B O A Θ P K Δ G X Σ
K A O Σ E A F Γ P O N I Z A A E
C M B V Γ K K Ω Σ A Φ A Ύ N P K
A A A I R O Π X O H Σ E K H T A
L E A A Σ O I A P Y O P A A A N
B E T K Σ P O R C U P I N E B S

BEAVER
BLACK BEAR
CHIPMUNK
CROCODILE
FROG
LLAMA
OPOSSUM
ORANGUTAN
OWL
PORCUPINE
RACCOON
RAT
SKUNK
SNAKE
SQUIRREL

ΚΑΣΤΟΡΑΣ
ΜΑΥΡΗ ΑΡΚΟΥΔΑ
ΣΚΙΟΥΡΑΚΙ
ΚΡΟΚΟΔΕΙΛΟΣ
ΒΑΤΡΑΧΟΣ
ΛΑΜΑ
ΟΠΟΣΟΥΜ
ΟΥΡΑΚΟΤΑΓΚΟΣ
ΚΟΥΚΟΥΒΑΓΙΑ
ΑΚΑΝΘΟΧΟΙΡΟΣ
ΡΑΚΟΥΝ
ΑΡΟΥΡΑΙΟΣ
ΠΑΛΙΆΝΘΡΩΠΟΣ
ΦΙΔΙ
ΣΚΙΟΥΡΟΣ

SEA LIFE

18

The blue whale is the largest animal on Earth. It's heart is the size of a car and can weigh as much as 50 elephants. Search the depths of the puzzle below for some other fascinating sea creatures.

E	Θ	H	T	N	B	E	A	N	H	A	D	M	H	O	Φ
T	A	O	T	U	C	C	H	S	I	F	Y	L	L	E	J
N	Λ	S	H	A	R	K	A	S	Φ	H	E	P	K	S	Ί
E	Ά	C	Λ	O	E	T	F	Σ	I	A	P	A	B	Q	X
T	Σ	N	R	Ά	T	I	L	O	T	F	Λ	L	T	U	E
Ю	Σ	O	W	A	S	N	C	E	S	A	R	A	O	I	Λ
Ά	I	I	A	H	B	T	K	Σ	M	A	K	A	I	D	Ω
E	O	L	L	M	O	V	A	A	A	E	R	O	T	N	N
S	Λ	A	R	P	L	K	P	E	H	I	H	O	Σ	S	A
P	I	E	U	O	P	I	X	H	I	Y	P	M	N	E	I
E	O	S	S	O	X	T	A	Π	O	Δ	I	E	Ά	A	K
G	N	E	A	H	Y	A	P	T	X	Y	O	Σ	T	L	Ω
S	T	M	Ώ	Δ	I	N	I	Φ	Λ	E	Δ	T	E	Σ	Φ
Я	Ά	I	P	Y	O	B	A	K	Я	E	Λ	Ί	T	I	A
I	P	Θ	A	Λ	A	Σ	Σ	I	O	Σ	I	Π	Π	O	Σ
W	I	P	A	Ψ	Ω	Ψ	M	E	I	A	E	L	A	H	W

TURTLE	ΧΕΛΩΝΑ
CRAB	ΚΑΒΟΥΡΙ
DOLPHIN	ΔΕΛΦΙΝΙ
FISH	ΨΑΡΙ
JELLYFISH	ΤΣΟΥΧΤΡΑ
LOBSTER	ΑΣΤΑΚΟΣ
OCTOPUS	ΧΤΑΠΟΔΙ
ORCA	ΟΡΚΑ
SEA LION	ΘΑΛΆΣΣΙΟ ΛΙΟΝΤΆΡΙ
SEAL	ΦΩΚΙΑ
SHARK	ΚΑΡΧΑΡΙΑΣ
SQUID	ΚΑΛΑΜΑΡΙ
STARFISH	ΑΣΤΕΡΙΑΣ
WALRUS	ΘΑΛΑΣΣΙΟΣ ΙΠΠΟΣ
WHALE	ΦΑΛΑΙΝΑ

FAMILY 1

Are you married? Do you have any siblings? Here is a list of terms that will help you to describe your nearest and dearest

A	N	H	Ψ	I	A	I	E	N	E	Γ	O	K	I	O
Ό	I	Π	A	I	Δ	I	A	I	Γ	A	I	Γ	C	B
G	M	E	X	A	E	R	I	S	L	X	I	T	E	A
R	Ψ	S	Θ	U	P	R	E	H	T	A	F	A	R	N
A	O	A	U	Γ	Φ	N	P	T	U	N	M	K	E	E
N	Π	A	Π	Π	O	Y	Σ	N	H	O	E	R	H	H
D	H	P	O	K	Σ	Σ	T	Γ	T	G	D	R	T	N
M	Ό	E	A	Ξ	A	R	O	H	Y	L	U	G	A	E
O	O	T	O	Δ	P	N	E	I	I	L	R	A	F	P
T	I	H	E	Γ	E	R	H	H	E	E	I	A	D	H
H	B	M	G	I	T	P	C	Ψ	T	Θ	H	M	N	E
E	E	Δ	Σ	O	A	M	Φ	S	I	O	R	Γ	A	W
R	E	G	E	Σ	Π	Y	I	H	I	O	R	Ό	R	F
Y	O	B	Ί	Δ	N	S	N	I	Ώ	A	Σ	B	G	Ά
L	T	V	N	I	E	C	E	L	C	N	U	Π	B	T

AUNT	ΘΕΙΑ
BROTHER	ΑΔΕΡΦΟΣ
CHILDREN	ΠΑΙΔΙΑ
DAUGHTER	ΚΟΡΗ
FAMILY	ΟΙΚΟΓΕΝΕΙΑ
FATHER	ΠΑΤΕΡΑΣ
GRANDFATHER	ΠΑΠΠΟΥΣ
GRANDMOTHER	ΓΙΑΓΙΑ
MOTHER	ΜΗΤΕΡΑ
NEPHEW	ΑΝΗΨΙΟΣ
NIECE	ΑΝΗΨΙΑ
PARENTS	ΓΟΝΕΙΣ
SISTER	ΑΔΕΡΦΗ
SON	ΓΙΟΣ
UNCLE	ΘΕΙΟΣ

FAMILY 2

Here are some more family members that you might be particularly fond of (or perhaps not)

G	I	W	G	T	Σ	O	Γ	Y	Z	Y	Σ	M	G	O	Д
A	G	R	A	N	D	S	O	N	I	F	Ω	R	E	B	I
Σ	G	I	R	L	A	P	R	U	A	P	A	K	O	Σ	Σ
O	D	Δ	C	G	N	Z	Z	T	O	N	O	Ю	A	O	T
P	T	A	O	Σ	Ψ	I	H	E	D	H	P	Γ	Δ	P	I
Π	E	S	U	Λ	O	E	R	D	Γ	O	Φ	A	A	E	P
M	G	F	S	G	R	Γ	A	E	Д	Γ	I	Y	I	Θ	O
A	R	H	I	I	H	U	Y	H	H	N	O	D	N	E	K
Γ	K	M	N	W	G	T	A	Z	Y	T	N	N	Y	Π	N
I	A	L	Ύ	H	A	Я	E	O	Y	A	O	B	O	U	H
Ώ	A	K	T	P	C	I	K	R	B	Σ	O	R	K	Σ	E
W	A	E	E	E	U	R	H	S	I	Y	B	A	B	Д	Γ
D	R	Θ	C	O	C	B	U	O	X	N	O	A	Φ	H	Γ
T	E	T	M	O	T	H	E	R	I	N	L	A	W	H	O
Π	P	T	T	A	H	S	O	N	I	N	L	A	W	Φ	N
A	Ю	T	S	I	S	T	E	R	I	N	L	A	W	O	H

BROTHER-IN-LAW	ΚΟΥΝΙΑΔΟΣ
BABY	ΜΩΡΟ
BOY	ΑΓΟΡΙ
COUSIN	ДВОЮРОДНАЯ СЕСТРА
DAUGHTER-IN-LAW	ΝΥΦΗ
FATHER-IN-LAW	ΠΕΘΕΡΟΣ
GIRL	ΚΟΡΙΤΣΙ
GRANDDAUGHTER	ΕΓΓΟΝΗ
GRANDSON	ΕΓΓΟΝΟΣ
HUSBAND	ΣΥΖΥΓΟΣ
MOTHER-IN-LAW	ΠΕΘΕΡΑ
SISTER-IN-LAW	ΚΟΥΝΙΑΔΑ
SON-IN-LAW	ΓΑΜΠΡΟΣ
WIFE	ΣΥΖΥΓΟΣ

VERBS 1

Actions speak louder than words. Here is a list of common verbs that you might encounter in your travels.

G M O E Y O H H R C O X E Д A
T N T T E P Δ A T T T Y D Π B
Ω O I T A S E W A T A R A O E
Y Ω A S Π H O E O B Q R E Θ G
E Λ W S O O O T L L T A R K N
P A O T K T H Π T S L C O Ί A
I B T K O I Ω P Λ A O O T T H
E Y U B N Π A K O H C T F T C
Γ O E K E Γ N Ό O O P E L O O
A K O Λ O Y Θ Ω T I S Ω E H T
M Ω B Y I Δ Π E P I M E N Ω O
Ω T Δ B Π A N Δ I A B A Z Ω P
Φ Ω Y O K A M A T E U B M Z A
Γ P P O T Ω W I Ω Z A Λ Λ A Y
T P T T N Ξ Σ K E Φ T O M A I

TO ASK	ΡΩΤΩ
TO BE	ΕΙΜΑΙ
TO CARRY	ΚΟΥΒΑΛΩ
TO CHANGE	ΑΛΛΑΖΩ
TO COOK	ΜΑΓΕΙΡΕΥΩ
TO EAT	ΤΡΩΩ
TO FOLLOW	ΑΚΟΛΟΥΘΩ
TO HEAR	ΑΚΟΥΩ
TO PAY	ΠΛΗΡΩΝΩ
TO READ	ΔΙΑΒΑΖΩ
TO SEE	ΒΛΕΠΩ
TO SING	ΤΡΑΓΟΥΔΩ
TO SLEEP	ΚΟΙΜΑΜΑΙ
TO THINK	ΣΚΕΦΤΟΜΑΙ
TO WAIT	ΠΕΡΙΜΕΝΩ

VERBS 2

There are thousands of verbs in use today. Here are some more popular verbs to practice. Find the translations below.

Ε	Χ	Ω	Α	Λ	Ι	Μ	C	Τ	Α	Χ	Ο	Ο	Α	Ι
Β	Ω	Ν	Ι	Α	Β	Α	Λ	Α	Τ	Α	Κ	Ύ	Π	Β
T	R	Y	C	H	E	Γ	Μ	Ω	Κ	Σ	Ι	Ρ	Β	Ο
G	O	T	E	M	H	A	Δ	Ο	Υ	Λ	Ε	Υ	Ω	Η
Ύ	F	T	O	Δ	D	Π	Ύ	Ψ	Χ	Ε	Ε	Ν	Κ	Θ
T	K	C	R	D	I	Ω	K	E	Y	P	X	I	A	Ω
T	O	N	A	A	O	Ξ	V	Ά	Θ	A	E	D	N	H
T	O	C	I	A	V	A	A	N	Ψ	N	N	P	Ω	Ω
T	L	S	L	R	H	E	A	T	T	I	I	E	T	Λ
O	O	N	P	O	D	T	L	O	F	A	Z	O	P	Y
T	T	H	T	E	S	O	S	O	Π	T	W	A	Ψ	O
A	N	L	E	O	A	E	T	O	L	O	V	E	S	Π
K	Z	N	T	L	L	K	B	N	R	Ω	Я	Д	E	I
E	E	N	O	L	P	N	P	K	T	E	H	X	T	N
E	T	O	U	N	D	E	R	S	T	A	N	D	T	Ω

TO CLOSE	ΚΛΕΙΝΩ
TO COME	ΕΡΧΟΜΑΙ
TO DO	ΚΑΝΩ
TO DRINK	ΠΙΝΩ
TO FIND	ΒΡΙΣΚΩ
TO HAVE	ΕΧΩ
TO HELP	ΒΟΗΘΩ
TO LOOK FOR	ΨΑΧΝΩ
TO LOVE	ΑΓΑΠΩ
TO SELL	ΠΟΥΛΩ
TO SPEAK	ΜΙΛΑΩ
TO TAKE	ΠΑΙΡΝΩ
TO TRAVEL	ΤΑΞΙΔΕΥΩ
TO UNDERSTAND	ΚΑΤΑΛΑΒΑΙΝΩ
TO WORK	ΔΟΥΛΕΥΩ

VERBS 3

23

Languages typically have a mix of regular and irregular verbs. A regular verb has a predictable conjugation. An irregular verb has a conjugation that does not follow the typical pattern. In English, many of the most common verbs are irregular.

X	S	A	H	Ω	M	T	P	E	X	Ω	Λ	E	Θ	D
Ω	P	M	I	R	Z	N	Ω	Γ	N	Ω	P	I	Z	Ω
Ω	B	Ω	R	N	R	I	Φ	I	Z	O	G	O	T	X
S	P	M	Σ	A	Θ	E	A	A	K	B	T	A	O	P
A	I	O	E	T	V	Θ	P	Π	N	E	Δ	P	Φ	P
A	Ό	L	Π	I	A	O	Γ	E	L	O	E	D	E	H
P	O	T	G	M	Γ	Ω	P	B	C	Y	I	X	Y	H
T	Ί	O	T	A	N	I	A	S	Ω	N	Y	Γ	Γ	N
O	T	W	E	I	S	E	T	N	T	A	A	Λ	Ω	U
O	Ю	R	Δ	V	B	N	I	W	A	H	L	D	T	R
P	E	I	Y	O	A	A	Ψ	O	Π	Γ	P	D	O	O
E	J	T	T	W	Γ	E	Ю	N	P	K	O	A	O	T
N	K	E	O	H	B	W	L	K	E	N	T	T	W	N
E	M	T	Π	T	Z	Δ	E	O	Π	Ξ	C	A	E	E
A	E	D	K	L	A	W	O	T	T	O	B	U	Y	Ί

TO BE ABLE TO	ΜΠΟΡΩ
TO BUY	ΑΓΟΡΑΖΩ
TO DANCE	ΧΟΡΕΥΩ
TO GIVE	ΔΙΝΩ
TO GO	ΠΗΓΑΙΝΩ
TO KNOW	ΓΝΩΡΙΖΩ
TO LEARN	ΜΑΘΑΙΝΩ
TO LEAVE	ΦΕΥΓΩ
TO OPEN	ΑΝΟΙΓΩ
TO OWE	ΧΡΩΣΤΑΩ
TO PLAY	ΠΑΙΖΩ
TO RUN	ΤΡΕΧΩ
TO WALK	ΠΕΡΠΑΤΩ
TO WANT	ΘΕΛΩ
TO WRITE	ΓΡΑΦΩ

FOOD 1

One of the greatures pleasures of travelling to another country is sampling the local cuisine. Study the word list below so you can order with confidence.

```
I Z Y P S F Λ A Σ U A Γ I A K
O R Y G A B A L O O E R A H P
P S G M W M X C K I M Ω Ψ Λ E
A E H P A X A Z O Φ P O Y T A
H L I T Λ P N E Λ N P Σ Γ Θ Σ
Ί B N P E M I W A Y A H S M Ю
U A B E Y A K K T Λ I U A T A
M T S P P T A Y A D G E Δ R A
A E E A I O O T O A A Φ W Y A
M G A S R B A Δ R E K L I M T
R E T T U B Λ Y S R E T A W R
Θ V N A O T Ύ E Γ B I I M S Ξ
H T O O L Z E Z C A E C N G A
T I U R F H O Ύ F A I O E B E
U Λ R Γ C H O C O L A T E Φ T
```

BREAD	ΨΩΜΙ
BUTTER	ΒΟΥΤΥΡΟ
CHEESE	ΤΥΡΙ
CHOCOLATE	ΣΟΚΟΛΑΤΑ
EGGS	ΑΥΓΑ
FLOUR	ΑΛΕΥΡΙ
FRUIT	ΦΡΟΥΤΑ
MEAT	ΚΡΕΑΣ
MILK	ΓΑΛΑ
PASTA	ΖΥΜΑΡΙΚΑ
RICE	ΡΥΖΙ
SALAD	ΣΑΛΑΤΑ
SUGAR	ΖΑΧΑΡΗ
VEGETABLES	ΛΑΧΑΝΙΚΑ
WATER	ΝΕΡΟ

FOOD 2

Want more? You have quite an appetite (for learning). Feast on this delicious buffet of mouth watering words.

T	Γ	Ά	A	R	Σ	O	Y	Π	A	F	A	Σ	K	Θ
Δ	G	K	K	E	T	T	Π	A	P	U	E	A	O	A
I	I	Σ	A	P	K	L	C	I	Y	Ύ	W	E	T	M
B	T	X	L	Z	N	N	A	W	Π	Д	W	P	O	Λ
Z	P	D	H	A	Ά	B	K	S	M	E	Y	K	Π	A
M	Y	E	M	L	M	Ά	E	T	T	O	P	O	O	A
L	O	X	Π	H	A	B	F	E	T	Ξ	O	I	Y	Ю
Λ	A	Δ	I	P	E	P	P	E	R	Π	T	Σ	Λ	Z
T	I	Θ	Σ	Σ	R	M	O	N	E	R	P	I	O	Λ
I	Γ	O	K	R	C	X	E	R	U	B	U	P	N	T
Ό	N	P	O	I	E	K	E	G	K	N	O	A	I	H
U	Ω	P	T	W	C	O	O	K	I	E	S	X	P	Ύ
O	Ό	A	A	I	I	Y	E	N	O	H	A	Σ	I	O
L	Λ	Ί	H	L	Ό	N	Π	A	Γ	Ω	T	O	O	M
A	N	C	H	K	X	T	E	B	I	Λ	E	M	X	N

BEEF	ΜΟΣΧΑΡΙΣΙΟ ΚΡΕΑΣ
BEER	ΜΠΥΡΑ
CAKE	ΤΟΥΡΤΑ
CHICKEN	ΚΟΤΟΠΟΥΛΟ
COOKIES	ΜΠΙΣΚΟΤΑ
HONEY	ΜΕΛΙ
ICE CREAM	ΠΑΓΩΤΟ
LAMB	ΑΡΝΙ
OIL	ΛΑΔΙ
PEPPER	ΠΙΠΕΡΙ
PORK	ΧΟΙΡΙΝΟ
SALT	ΑΛΑΤΙ
SOUP	ΣΟΥΠΑ
WINE	ΚΡΑΣΙ
YOGURT	ΓΙΑΟΥΡΤΙ

FRUIT 1

26

A fruit is the part of a plant that surrounds the seeds, whereas a vegetable is a plant that has some other edible part. Tomatoes, cucumbers and peppers are three examples of fruit that are often classified as vegetables.

H Д O U I N O N H K Σ A M A Δ A
T Y O P Φ Π I E P K Γ Y I A I N
P O Δ A K I N O Θ W P N T Δ E A
K A P Π O Y Z I A T O I A S I N
L B H S T V O T I Π U Λ E O Λ A
P E E C T Φ E Λ E R X I G Σ A Σ
R O L M A R O Π F A R I G T K O
N T M P M E A E A R T N P A O K
M O X E P E P W E E O O L Φ T O
M U L P G A P B B N C M A Y P K
D O E E R R E E S E I E N Λ O I
N A M G M U A N G E R Λ T I Π P
R Ώ O K L O E N I N P R I A E E
O Θ N B X M I Λ A P A A I Δ W B
M Σ E Λ Y O A P Φ T E R R E O H
C A N A Z T I Λ E M E L O G S P

APRICOT	ΒΕΡΙΚΟΚΟ
BLUEBERRIES	ΜΥΡΤΙΛΟ
EGGPLANT	ΜΕΛΙΤΖΑΝΑ
GRAPEFRUIT	ΓΚΡΕΙΠΦΡΟΥΤ
GRAPES	ΣΤΑΦΥΛΙΑ
LEMON	ΛΕΜΟΝΙ
MELON	ΠΕΠΟΝΙ
ORANGE	ΠΟΡΤΟΚΑΛΙ
PEACH	ΡΟΔΑΚΙΝΟ
PEAR	ΑΧΛΑΔΙ
PINEAPPLE	ΑΝΑΝΑΣ
PLUM	ΔΑΜΑΣΚΗΝΟ
POMEGRANATE	ΡΟΔΙ
STRAWBERRIES	ΦΡΑΟΥΛΕΣ
WATERMELON	ΚΑΡΠΟΥΖΙ

FRUIT 2

There are more than 7000 different varieties of apples being grown around the world today. Check out our produce section below for some more fresh and tasty fruit.

```
E K O D Δ R Σ A B H Д P H E A S S
A I P E Π I Π H N I K K O K N E K
O A R A A Θ Y K O Λ O K A I I I I
A I P Θ E O H B L Λ T N K R S R T
X P Σ Y E R M S O I T P R E E R P
E E Y K O I E K A A M E A P I E I
E Π K O A E Y D Λ U B E P P R B N
Ύ I O Λ M Θ M O P P Q E P E R K H
E Π A O A O Y Σ S E P S L P E C Π
T H W K O Π T A Z W P T E N H A I
E N I M E M R A O U Z P Δ E C L Π
A I Σ A P E K L B B C I E E A B E
O Σ E P U O L A T N A C E R A Ί P
Λ A K R Ί E A T E S O N H G R O I
H P A O Y V M Ά P T A Y A I I B A
M Π A N A N A T A M O T N N N F E
T O M A T O T T H H Y N Ξ H A I H
```

APPLE	ΜΗΛΟ
BANANA	ΜΠΑΝΑΝΑ
BLACKBERRIES	ΒΑΤΟΜΟΥΡΑ
CANTALOUPE	ΚΑΝΤΑΛΟΥΠΕ
CHERRIES	ΚΕΡΑΣΙΑ
FIG	ΣΥΚΟ
GREEN PEPPER	ΠΡΑΣΙΝΗ ΠΙΠΕΡΙΑ
LIME	ΛΑΙΜ
PUMPKIN	ΚΟΛΟΚΥΘΑ
RASPBERRIES	ΣΜΕΟΥΡΑ
RED PEPPER	ΚΟΚΚΙΝΗ ΠΙΠΕΡΙΑ
SQUASH	ΚΟΛΟΚΥΘΑ
TOMATO	ΝΤΟΜΑΤΑ
YELLOW PEPPER	ΚΙΤΡΙΝΗ ΠΙΠΕΡΙΑ
ZUCCHINI	ΚΟΛΟΚΥΘΑΚΙ

VEGETABLES 1

28

A 2013 study estimated that up to 87% of people in the United States do no consume their daily recommended portion of vegetables. Here is a list of vegetables that you should probably be eating more of.

```
K O Y I M P O T A T O E S E O Λ
T A Ί Λ L X T S S S D Ψ G I E K
R Ύ P Y E Φ C K P S T A E Ю A C
H K O O W Ά P A A I B E L L O A
Λ Σ Π P T E H E R B N E E N Y U
A K S A M O P Σ A T T A H B R L
X O O M T N Π C G T I Π C O E I
A P Y Y E A M O U C A C N H L F
N Δ H E N Δ T C S N I I H O E L
I O R A H O E E T R Λ L C O C O
Δ G K Ά R T Y Z Σ E T C R R K W
A I Γ Γ A P A Π Σ T O R R A C E
O Λ O K O P Π M I R F X P U G R
A P A N I K Γ A B Δ T O N I O N
O Π P A Σ I N A M Π I Z E Λ I A
I A E H M M G Λ A X A N O E M T
```

ARTICHOKE	ΑΓΚΙΝΑΡΑ
ASPARAGUS	ΣΠΑΡΑΓΓΙΑ
BEETS	ΠΑΝΤΖΑΡΙΑ
BROCCOLI	ΜΠΡΟΚΟΛΟ
CABBAGE	ΛΑΧΑΝΟ
CARROT	ΚΑΡΟΤΟ
CAULIFLOWER	ΚΟΥΝΟΥΠΙΔΙ
CELERY	ΣΕΛΙΝΟ
GARLIC	ΣΚΟΡΔΟ
GREEN PEAS	ΠΡΑΣΙΝΑ ΜΠΙΖΕΛΙΑ
KALE	ΛΑΧΑΝΙΔΑ
LETTUCE	ΜΑΡΟΥΛΙ
ONION	ΚΡΕΜΜΥΔΙ
POTATOES	ΠΑΤΑΤΕΣ
SPINACH	ΣΠΑΝΑΚΙ

HOUSE

There's no place like home. Below is a list of words that are related to house and home.

Γ	Μ	Π	Α	Ν	Ι	Ο	Ζ	Η	Η	Ε	Τ	Ν	Ι	Ε	G
Ώ	K	D	I	K	I	T	C	H	E	N	C	W	I	T	I
Η	Σ	Α	Λ	Ο	Ν	Ι	Ά	Υ	Ε	G	Ξ	Ν	Ρ	Θ	Γ
Ν	Δ	Θ	Ρ	D	Δ	Ι	Α	Μ	Σ	W	Α	Α	Ε	Α	Κ
Κ	Ρ	Ε	Β	Α	Τ	Ι	Ε	Ρ	Ο	Η	Π	R	Ρ	F	Ι
Ο	Ο	D	Α	Ι	Ζ	S	Α	D	Α	Ε	Τ	Α	Α	Μ	Θ
Υ	Μ	Ο	Π	Α	Α	D	Ν	Μ	Ζ	R	Μ	Χ	Ο	G	F
Ζ	Α	Σ	D	B	L	I	I	A	E	A	T	O	A	T	F
I	K	K	Π	R	W	I	P	N	K	P	R	M	A	P	A
N	I	E	A	Y	I	I	E	O	I	G	I	B	E	Ί	Φ
Α	Δ	Π	Ρ	Π	Α	V	T	S	N	N	Ο	Σ	Ε	Ν	Η
G	I	Η	Α	Ο	Д	Α	Ε	Ι	U	Ε	G	Ι	Μ	Ω	Τ
Я	Σ	Μ	Θ	Γ	Β	Ώ	V	W	F	O	O	R	I	A	Φ
O	A	G	Y	E	Ώ	I	R	B	A	T	H	R	O	O	M
I	Ρ	Γ	Ρ	I	L	A	W	N	Z	Y	B	H	M	O	I
Ρ	Γ	K	O	O	G	L	D	E	B	E	D	R	O	O	M

APARTMENT	ΔΙΑΜΕΡΙΣΜΑ
BASEMENT	ΥΠΟΓΕΙΟ
BATHROOM	ΜΠΑΝΙΟ
BED	ΚΡΕΒΑΤΙ
BEDROOM	ΚΡΕΒΑΤΟΚΑΜΑΡΑ
DINING ROOM	ΤΡΑΠΕΖΑΡΙΑ
DRIVEWAY	ΔΡΟΜΑΚΙ
FENCE	ΦΡΑΧΤΗΣ
GARAGE	ΓΚΑΡΑΖ
HOUSE	ΣΠΙΤΙ
KITCHEN	ΚΟΥΖΙΝΑ
LAWN	ΓΡΑΣΙΔΙ
LIVING ROOM	ΣΑΛΟΝΙ
ROOF	ΣΚΕΠΗ
WINDOW	ΠΑΡΑΘΥΡΟ

AROUND THE HOUSE 1

It is estimated that one tenth of all furniture purchased in Britain comes from IKEA. Perhaps you have assembled a few of these items yourself.

P	E	Z	B	C	H	O	U	F	H	B	A	Π	M	A	Λ
A	M	U	U	C	A	V	I	Σ	K	A	Λ	E	Σ	A	A
H	P	A	Ό	R	N	R	H	T	P	A	Π	E	Z	I	E
C	M	E	L	Θ	E	Σ	P	E	X	O	R	L	S	Σ	N
H	N	N	I	P	Y	S	I	E	I	T	A	T	O	T	I
A	F	I	L	P	I	N	S	P	T	N	A	I	A	E	H
N	I	A	B	Z	A	C	H	E	I	I	A	Π	Λ	Γ	C
D	C	T	U	Π	O	T	S	T	R	Λ	I	I	X	N	A
E	Φ	R	M	C	N	T	P	S	E	D	K	Σ	A	Ω	M
L	E	U	Y	Y	E	Y	A	Y	Φ	H	A	I	Λ	T	G
I	L	C	Λ	L	O	T	Λ	Ό	Σ	T	Z	N	I	H	N
E	B	Π	I	K	T	O	Y	A	Λ	E	T	A	N	P	I
R	A	O	L	R	Π	Λ	B	A	T	H	T	U	B	I	H
K	T	C	Y	D	R	Y	E	R	M	S	P	B	H	O	S
B	Y	L	O	O	P	G	N	I	M	M	I	W	S	B	A
A	Π	Y	O	K	Σ	H	K	I	P	T	K	E	Λ	H	W

BATHTUB	ΜΠΑΝΙΕΡΑ
CARPET	ΧΑΛΙ
CHANDELIER	ΠΟΛΥΕΛΑΙΟΣ
CURTAIN	ΚΟΥΡΤΙΝΑ
DRESSER	ΣΥΡΤΑΡΙΕΡΑ
DRYER	ΣΤΕΓΝΩΤΗΡΙΟ
FAUCET	ΒΡΥΣΗ
FIREPLACE	ΤΖΑΚΙ
LAMP	ΛΑΜΠΑ
SWIMMING POOL	ΠΙΣΙΝΑ
STAIRS	ΣΚΑΛΕΣ
TABLE	ΤΡΑΠΕΖΙ
TOILET	ΤΟΥΑΛΕΤΑ
VACUUM	ΗΛΕΚΤΡΙΚΗ ΣΚΟΥΠΑ
WASHING MACHINE	ΠΛΥΝΤΗΡΙΟ

AROUND THE HOUSE 2

Here is a list of some more common household items and modern conveniences. Search the grid for the words listed below

A A R Θ P A N I O I E Γ Y Ψ X N K

Δ N N O V E N H X K C A W O Ω O G

A E E A T E S O L C R I B T Y O Λ

N Y P M M A T T R E S S A N N H Σ

I A O Ω I I R E M K U I I Z H Y O

M T X P O Σ W E A A Π A Λ Y O T N

A M Y T R O T Θ G O Ξ I Φ T S I P

K T T Σ H E P H I I C I N L B Ω Y

A Ψ H S N E H P P E R H Λ Z E L O

P I Σ V Φ M H S I A A F I A O I Φ

E S Ψ T Ώ T N L A L Σ Д E M P N I

K O H B N Z I A L W Ω O A R N I O

Λ Σ C Y T N H W O S H T P K S E D

A I Λ H G H A L T U Y S S O Ω F Y

H Π Ά F A Y L O R O R R I M Φ Ю T

E O A N I I X O T O Y Ό N D M H E

O N Ю O P T R P V H O Y K Ω M A Σ

CHAIR	ΚΑΡΕΚΛΑ
CEILING FAN	ΑΝΕΜΙΣΤΗΡΑΣ ΟΡΟΦΗΣ
CHIMNEY	ΚΑΜΙΝΑΔΑ
CLOSET	ΝΤΟΥΛΑΠΑ
CRIB	ΚΟΥΝΙΑ
DESK	ΘΡΑΝΙΟ
DISHWASHER	ΠΛΥΝΤΗΡΙΟ ΠΙΑΤΩΝ
HALLWAY	ΧΟΛ
MATTRESS	ΣΤΡΩΜΑ
MIRROR	ΚΑΘΡΕΦΤΗΣ
OVEN	ΦΟΥΡΝΟΣ
PILLOW	ΜΑΞΙΛΑΡΙ
REFRIGERATOR	ΨΥΓΕΙΟ
SHOWER	ΝΤΟΥΣ
SINK	ΝΕΡΟΧΥΤΗΣ

AT THE TABLE

32

Table setting etiquette dictates that the forks be placed on the left hand side of the plate and knives on the right. Here are some items that you might find on your table, probably in the wrong location.

Σ	A	Π	Y	O	Σ	Σ	H	T	I	Λ	A	T	Y	O	K
H	T	R	E	P	P	E	P	N	U	A	R	Ю	I	Λ	A
M	E	W	M	P	I	Ύ	Y	T	Λ	E	E	A	I	H	P
H	Σ	I	U	Δ	L	O	L	A	H	T	H	Σ	N	T	A
G	T	N	G	Ώ	P	A	T	C	A	Ί	A	O	E	N	Φ
P	E	E	O	H	S	I	T	A	S	P	O	Π	Π	A	A
Y	Π	G	Π	O	I	I	Λ	E	K	P	V	E	Y	M	Λ
M	O	L	N	Ώ	P	P	N	A	S	S	A	L	G	O	E
P	T	A	O	Ά	Ю	S	I	A	T	Π	U	E	Π	Z	K
Ό	P	S	O	I	R	Γ	E	A	P	Y	I	M	A	E	E
I	A	S	P	F	I	T	F	L	X	K	O	Π	Δ	Π	A
I	X	C	S	P	O	T	I	W	B	A	I	K	E	A	E
Π	O	T	H	P	I	R	N	O	N	A	M	N	K	P	H
Φ	O	T	A	I	Π	R	K	B	R	O	T	N	C	T	I
K	O	Y	T	A	Λ	I	T	O	Y	Γ	Λ	Y	K	O	Y
Π	B	T	A	B	L	E	C	L	O	T	H	A	M	E	S

BOWL	ΜΠΟΛ
FORK	ΠΗΡΟΥΝΙ
GLASS	ΠΟΤΗΡΙ
KNIFE	ΜΑΧΑΙΡΙ
MUG	ΚΟΥΠΑ
NAPKIN	ΧΑΡΤΟΠΕΤΣΕΤΑ
PEPPER	ΠΙΠΕΡΙ
PITCHER	ΚΑΡΑΦΑ
PLATE	ΠΙΑΤΟ
SALT	ΑΛΑΤΙ
SPOON	ΚΟΥΤΑΛΙ
TABLECLOTH	ΤΡΑΠΕΖΟΜΑΝΤΗΛΟ
TABLESPOON	ΚΟΥΤΑΛΙ ΤΗΣ ΣΟΥΠΑΣ
TEASPOON	ΚΟΥΤΑΛΙ ΤΟΥ ΓΛΥΚΟΥ
WINE GLASS	ΠΟΤΗΡΙ ΓΙΑ ΚΡΑΣΙ

TOOLS

Time to get out the tool box and do some repairs on our vocabulary. Try to hammer a few of these words and their translations into you brain.

B	Ύ	Ί	O	Ξ	E	N	P	Ω	B	O	L	T	R	A
Z	A	T	H	S	W	P	H	C	N	E	R	W	E	L
N	O	Λ	Z	H	Γ	A	K	U	V	P	A	S	D	R
M	P	W	A	Π	B	A	T	E	Д	S	K	R	E	T
T	T	Σ	C	K	Σ	I	L	P	H	I	I	Z	R	A
E	E	D	Δ	N	Σ	S	R	E	I	L	P	E	E	P
Π	M	Λ	E	M	Φ	Ύ	R	N	L	N	D	Θ	V	E
A	S	Π	K	O	Y	T	P	C	H	D	N	S	I	M
Ξ	B	A	O	Λ	P	T	Z	I	A	A	S	S	R	E
I	I	Λ	Γ	Y	I	D	Y	L	I	T	M	A	D	A
M	Δ	Φ	Π	B	Λ	A	I	L	M	R	O	M	W	S
A	A	A	P	I	P	O	Δ	E	Λ	A	I	K	E	U
Δ	N	Δ	E	A	R	I	N	O	I	P	Π	E	R	R
I	Δ	I	E	Λ	K	O	K	I	Λ	Λ	A	Γ	C	E
K	A	T	Σ	A	B	I	Δ	I	W	E	R	C	S	N

BOLT	ΜΠΟΥΛΟΝΙ
DRILL	ΤΡΥΠΑΝΙ
HAMMER	ΣΦΥΡΙ
LADDER	ΣΚΑΛΑ
LEVEL	ΑΛΦΑΔΙ
NAIL	ΚΑΡΦΙ
NUT	ΠΑΞΙΜΑΔΙ
PENCIL	ΜΟΛΥΒΙ
PLIERS	ΠΕΝΣΑ
SAW	ΠΡΙΟΝΙ
SCREW	ΒΙΔΑ
SCREWDRIVER	ΚΑΤΣΑΒΙΔΙ
TAPE MEASURE	ΜΕΤΡΟ
WASHER	ΡΟΔΕΛΑ
WRENCH	ΓΑΛΛΙΚΟ ΚΛΕΙΔΙ

CLOTHES 1

34

Globally there are 1.2 billion pairs of jeans sold annually. That is a lot of denim! Take a look at this list of other common articles of clothing.

A R Ά S X I N O Λ E T N A Π N
M E O H A V E S T Λ Θ B Π T Y
F T A O C Ί O Ά B O H Γ A N M
Я A F R A C S A Д S U I Λ O I
E E I T K C E N Σ P N Λ T Λ M
S W S S E R D B A T I E O E Π
S S T N A P N J O K P K R Π A
S E A Σ K Γ A Q A R Σ O O A Π
O V O B E M A Λ Ά A H Y Σ K O
Ξ O E H A M T N K O Λ T A H Y
T L M S S Σ A R T O A M A H T
T G R M E I B Z B I E T N B Σ
E Ψ I Σ N N A E T P A Ω A E I
K Z M Π O Y P N O Y Z I J N A
I R F H M O Γ Φ T N Π O T S V

BATHROBE
BELT
COAT
DRESS
GLOVES
HAT
NECKTIE
PAJAMAS
PANTS
SCARF
SHOES
SHORTS
SOCKS
SWEATER
VEST

ΜΠΟΥΡΝΟΥΖΙ
ΖΩΝΗ
ΠΑΛΤΟ
ΦΟΡΕΜΑ
ΓΑΝΤΙΑ
ΚΑΠΕΛΟ
ΓΡΑΒΑΤΑ
ΠΥΤΖΑΜΕΣ
ΠΑΝΤΕΛΟΝΙ
ΚΑΣΚΟΛ
ΠΑΠΟΥΤΣΙΑ
ΣΟΡΤΣ
ΚΑΛΤΣΕΣ
ΠΟΥΛΟΒΕΡ
ΓΙΛΕΚΟ

CLOTHES 2

More than 2 billion t-shirts are sold each year! How many of these other items can be found in your closet?

E	V	O	N	O	I	H	C	T	A	W	T	S	I	R	W
Λ	X	Ю	N	E	A	O	M	I	E	E	H	U	T	M	E
Σ	Θ	H	W	Ό	C	Z	Ξ	S	W	I	M	S	U	I	T
E	Z	S	T	R	I	K	S	Ω	R	T	S	P	L	T	M
T	B	O	O	T	S	Y	L	T	Ω	W	L	E	U	E	I
O	I	R	Ю	D	A	E	T	A	I	O	A	N	Ω	X	T
Π	Π	P	A	O	N	M	Ψ	M	C	B	D	D	O	E	I
M	Φ	Я	A	C	Π	J	Y	A	E	E	N	E	Σ	A	Σ
A	N	O	I	N	E	O	C	Δ	R	O	A	R	A	B	O
Γ	E	R	Y	A	T	L	Y	W	N	H	S	S	N	P	Y
I	Y	I	N	Σ	O	E	E	K	Φ	E	U	E	Δ	A	T
O	Ύ	S	Y	T	T	A	Σ	T	A	I	Γ	V	A	X	I
Ώ	A	O	H	N	R	A	P	Ω	T	M	K	O	Λ	I	E
T	K	I	Y	B	T	E	H	Π	A	Π	I	Γ	I	O	N
C	N	P	O	Λ	O	I	X	E	I	P	O	Σ	A	Λ	I
G	P	Ό	S	Ψ	H	E	Σ	Ω	P	O	Y	X	O	I	Π

WRIST WATCH	ΡΟΛΟΙ ΧΕΙΡΟΣ
BOOTS	ΜΠΟΤΕΣ
BOW TIE	ΠΑΠΙΓΙΟΝ
BRA	ΣΟΥΤΙΕΝ
BRACELET	ΒΡΑΧΙΟΛΙ
CLOTHING	ΕΝΔΥΜΑ
JEANS	ΤΖΗΝ
NECKLACE	ΚΟΛΙΕ
SANDALS	ΣΑΝΔΑΛΙΑ
SHIRT	ΠΟΥΚΑΜΙΣΟ
SKIRT	ΦΟΥΣΤΑ
SUIT	ΚΟΥΣΤΟΥΜΙ
SUSPENDERS	ΤΙΡΑΝΤΕΣ
SWIM SUIT	ΜΑΓΙΟ
UNDERWEAR	ΕΣΩΡΟΥΧΟ

GETTING READY

36

The majority of people take less than half an hour to get ready in the morning. Some can be ready in less than 5 minutes, whereas some take over an hour. Here is a list of things that might be a part of your morning routine.

P A T E N K O N T I Σ I O N E P H

W T M K C I T S P I L Δ X Y A E B

R Σ K Y Π A M E P K O T N O Δ O M

Ύ H P A Λ A H E S N O C Φ B Γ S O

Σ Φ A A S A K X T H X T E N A S C

A A Γ I Σ H I I H S A W H T U O M

M Π I R T T K Δ E A Σ M N Γ N L Σ

Π E O Ώ E O P T O M I A P T P F A

O I N Σ N N P Y O K R R A O A L Π

Y O Σ H M E O I O O I C D C O A O

A K M T R H K I D B T T R R S T Y

N A K F O A T O T L O H A O Y N N

C Φ U Ω Φ Λ E I E I M T B M E E I

A M N A Π D A N K Я D Π N R O D R

E A P Ω M A S K K O O N Φ O U T K

S Y M A K E U P I R A Z O R Δ S Σ

Ξ W E T S A P H T O O T T C A O H

COMB	XTENA
CONDITIONER	KONTIΣIONEP
CONTACT LENSES	ΦAKOI EΠAΦHΣ
DENTAL FLOSS	OΔONTIKO NHMA
DEODORANT	AΠOΣMHTIKO
HAIR DRYER	ΠIΣTOΛAKI
LIPSTICK	KPAΓION
MAKEUP	MEIKAΠ
MOUTHWASH	ΣTOMATIKO ΔIAΛYMA
PERFUME	APΩMA
RAZOR	ΞYPAΦAKI
SHAMPOO	ΣAMΠOYAN
SOAP	ΣAΠOYNI
TOOTHBRUSH	OΔONTOBOYPTΣA
TOOTHPASTE	OΔONTOKPEMA

PLACES 1

Places to go and people to see. Here are some places that you might visit around town.

```
I D T U T H O S P I T A L H Я P I
C Z N R D E U O I E M O K O Σ O N
E E E A A S K C I O O I T N B T Φ
S P M Σ B I E P Y Δ T Ω O N A A Π
U O T A I K N Σ A Σ A I O X P O E
O S R E H Δ E S E M T T Y O Λ I Θ
H T A K K I H B T A P Δ Σ Y M E N
T O P I O R Σ P T A P E K Γ T Φ P
H F E H R O A S O O T A Π A Ψ A Y
G F D G P P E M M Δ T I A Y Π P X
I I Δ Y D R O E R A P M O M O Γ O
L C Π O I I I R Σ E P O T N T Σ I
O E T F O O R T T A P Y M F T Π E
O Σ X F Ξ Ό H B Φ U S U Φ I O T Λ
H Д O I Ύ M M U I D A T S E K B O
C Ψ H C A E P O Δ P O M I O Γ O X
S A Δ E R E H M U E S U M R A F Σ
```

AIRPORT	ΑΕΡΟΔΡΟΜΙΟ
BAR	ΜΠΑΡ
BRIDGE	ΓΕΦΥΡΑ
DEPARTMENT store	ΠΟΛΥΚΑΤΑΣΤΗΜΑ
FARM	ΦΑΡΜΑ
FIRE STATION	ΠΥΡΟΣΒΕΣΤΙΚΗ
HOSPITAL	ΝΟΣΟΚΟΜΕΙΟ
LIGHTHOUSE	ΦΑΡΟΣ
MUSEUM	ΜΟΥΣΕΙΟ
OFFICE	ΓΡΑΦΕΙΟ
POST OFFICE	ΤΑΧΥΔΡΟΜΕΙΟ
SCHOOL	ΣΧΟΛΕΙΟ
STADIUM	ΣΤΑΔΙΟ
SUPERMARKET	ΣΟΥΠΕΡΜΑΡΚΕΤ
TRAIN STATION	ΣΙΔΗΡΟΔΡΟΜΙΚΟΣ σταθμοσ

PLACES 2

38

The weekend is finally here. Where to you feel like going tonight? Here are some more places you can visit.

```
A I P E T E Φ A K Ξ K E L T S A C
T Σ A C Γ P G F E O N K Ψ N Ύ O E
Π N T O O O A N Y C A M R A H P M
R A O Y Y F O Π R N B H N A O R E
H O N H N Δ F Я E Ώ T E A L P S T
H R O E O O P E A Z K H I R U X E
K O E X Π E M S E P A C E O B H R
H O E S O I O I O S E C H A S O Y
Θ I E I T K Σ T K S H A Ψ O T T R
O P A N P A A T T O R O P I O E A
I O M A Ό Φ U A H E T T P E R L R
Λ T Π M E T T R P M Σ M J K E E B
B A C I F I I O A A I I H A I J I
I I O Λ O R T Ί K N Σ O O M O Θ L
B T U N I V E R S I T Y Ί P A E H
K Σ O Π E P A M H T Σ A T A K T S
Θ E A T P O T S T O O U K Φ N X T
```

BANK	ΤΡΑΠΕΖΑ
CASTLE	ΚΑΣΤΡΟ
CEMETERY	ΝΕΚΡΟΤΑΦΕΙΟ
COFFEE SHOP	ΚΑΦΕΤΕΡΙΑ
HARBOR	ΛΙΜΑΝΙ
HOTEL	ΞΕΝΟΔΟΧΕΙΟ
LIBRARY	ΒΙΒΛΙΟΘΗΚΗ
OPERA HOUSE	ΟΠΕΡΑ
PARK	ΠΑΡΚΟ
PHARMACY	ΦΑΡΜΑΚΕΙΟ
POLICE STATION	ΑΣΤΥΝΟΜΙΚΟ ΤΜΗΜΑ
RESTAURANT	ΕΣΤΙΑΤΟΡΙΟ
STORE	ΚΑΤΑΣΤΗΜΑ
THEATER	ΘΕΑΤΡΟ
UNIVERSITY	ΠΑΝΕΠΙΣΤΗΜΙΟ

ON THE ROAD

Road trip time! Hop in your car, turn up the music and hit the open road. Make sure you study this list of road worthy translations before heading out.

I H R O I E P O Φ Ω E Λ Ω P I Δ A
P N Σ S Γ R O T H N I K O T Y A U
A I O H Π A J M O N O Δ P O M O Σ
N Z T N N I H H I B C R I B K A T
A N H S E I N O A I U E U I W R O
Φ E T M K W K A F C P S Δ O A N L
C B G U O H A F K O C A S F Z G G
Д O K A E T A Y Φ I N I F T A I N
X Ψ Γ Д S R O Ω S I Δ I D U O S I
U A N H T S E Σ Z T C A T E T P K
Δ M I A T Λ T N Y L R O Σ R N O R
P H K Y H P E A I K M E U T Ώ T A
O X P Σ P B O G T O Λ C E R O S P
M Y A B O R H Φ B I K E Ю T E Π P
O T Π T K T Z I D A O R T D Y O A
Σ A G A S O L I N E H N N A Δ E N
Ό H L A N E L C Y C R O T O M Σ R

AUTOMOBILE	ΑΥΤΟΚΙΝΗΤΟ
ACCIDENT	ΑΤΥΧΗΜΑ
BUS	ΛΕΩΦΟΡΕΙΟ
BUS STOP	ΣΤΑΣΗ ΛΕΩΦΟΡΕΙΟΥ
GAS STATION	ΒΕΝΖΙΝΑΔΙΚΟ
GASOLINE	ΒΕΝΖΙΝΗ
LANE	ΛΩΡΙΔΑ
MOTORCYCLE	ΜΟΤΟΣΥΚΛΕΤΑ
ONE-WAY STREET	ΜΟΝΟΔΡΟΜΟΣ
PARKING LOT	ΠΑΡΚΙΝΓΚ
ROAD	ΔΡΟΜΟΣ
STOP SIGN	ΠΙΝΑΚΙΔΑ ΣΤΟΠ
TRAFFIC LIGHT	ΦΑΝΑΡΙ
TRAFFIC	ΚΙΝΗΣΗ
TRUCK	ΦΟΡΤΗΓΟ

GETTING AROUND

There are many interesting ways of getting from A to B. Which mode of transportation will you choose?

Π Z A L I S U B L O O H C S O Σ E

E Y E Σ X H O E L C Y C I B X Ύ E

Ί E P X O A O E N Σ K A Φ O Σ E Ό

T A O O T M M V Λ I B Ώ Λ N T E C

A I Π B Σ A O B E I R I Y A M Y F

Ά I Λ E O B N P K R K A T K T A H

A K A P T T E K Δ O C O M O H W Π

Σ Y N K A L E Σ Λ O H R Π B R B E

Θ Π O P Λ X A E T E P M A T U U P

E O N A H C Ω I L I I H A F E S I

N B E Φ Δ Φ A I R P K N Δ A T P Π

O P P T O P C N E P K O Σ I K T O

Φ Y T P Π O Ί Φ O Σ L C O O Σ Y Λ

O X E N P O L I C E C A R X R R I

P I O T G Σ E E T R A I N R H C K

O O E C N A L U B M A A E E Ω M O

A R W K C U R T E R I F E R Ω B A

AIRPLANE	ΑΕΡΟΠΛΑΝΟ
AMBULANCE	ΑΣΘΕΝΟΦΟΡΟ
BICYCLE	ΠΟΔΗΛΑΤΟ
BOAT	ΣΚΑΦΟΣ
CANOE	ΚΑΝΟ
FERRY	ΦΕΡΙΜΠΟΤ
FIRE TRUCK	ΠΥΡΟΣΒΕΣΤΙΚΟ ΟΧΗΜΑ
HELICOPTER	ΕΛΙΚΟΠΤΕΡΟ
HOVERCRAFT	ΧΟΒΕΡΚΡΑΦΤ
POLICE CAR	ΠΕΡΙΠΟΛΙΚΟ
SCHOOL BUS	ΣΧΟΛΙΚΟ ΛΕΩΦΟΡΕΙΟ
SUBMARINE	ΥΠΟΒΡΥΧΙΟ
SUBWAY	υπογειοσ ΣΙΔΗΡΟΔΡΟΜΟΣ
TANK	ΤΑΝΚΣ
TRAIN	ΤΡΕΝΟ

LANGUAGES 1

Here are some popular languages from around the world. Maybe you already know one or two of them.

Π	A	A	E	S	E	M	A	N	T	E	I	V	Д	A	G
W	Z	Ί	A	K	I	Λ	A	Γ	O	T	P	O	Π	A	R
E	N	A	K	I	N	Ω	Λ	O	Π	A	A	T	K	K	E
R	M	A	N	Δ	A	P	I	N	I	K	A	I	O	I	E
B	A	K	I	N	A	Π	Σ	I	I	Y	Z	E	P	Λ	K
E	Λ	I	K	A	P	A	Ω	N	N	E	T	Λ	E	Γ	Я
H	I	B	S	O	K	O	A	N	M	Φ	P	Λ	A	Γ	Ώ
S	T	A	Ί	I	R	M	R	A	E	K	E	H	T	A	E
S	L	P	Λ	N	P	E	N	T	E	Z	N	N	I	Λ	O
L	P	A	I	E	I	T	A	E	U	B	I	I	K	Λ	P
Φ	T	A	Γ	T	E	R	N	N	N	G	P	K	A	I	Ω
I	Z	R	N	I	A	X	A	Y	A	G	U	A	A	K	Σ
I	Z	A	B	I	O	L	E	D	T	M	L	E	I	A	I
H	Я	B	R	U	S	S	I	A	N	N	R	I	S	K	K
H	S	I	L	O	P	H	J	A	P	A	N	E	S	E	A
R	H	C	N	E	R	F	Φ	Ά	N	A	M	U	G	H	Ψ

ARABIC	APABIKA
ENGLISH	ΑΓΓΛΙΚΑ
FRENCH	ΓΑΛΛΙΚΑ
GERMAN	ΓΕΡΜΑΝΙΚΑ
GREEK	ΕΛΛΗΝΙΚΑ
ITALIAN	ΙΤΑΛΙΚΑ
JAPANESE	ΙΑΠΩΝΕΖΙΚΑ
KOREAN	ΚΟΡΕΑΤΙΚΑ
MANDARIN	ΜΑΝΔΑΡΙΝΙΚΑ
POLISH	ΠΟΛΩΝΙΚΑ
PORTUGUESE	ΠΟΡΤΟΓΑΛΙΚΑ
RUSSIAN	ΡΩΣΙΚΑ
SPANISH	ΙΣΠΑΝΙΚΑ
HEBREW	ΕΒΡΑΙΚΑ
VIETNAMESE	ΒΙΕΤΝΑΜΕΖΙΚΑ

PROFESSIONS

Statistics suggest that the average person may change careers 5-7 times in their lives. Thinking about a change? Why not try one of these great professions?

Ά	I	Σ	Ώ	R	O	T	C	A	R	P	E	N	T	E	R	K
E	Δ	G	O	M	F	I	R	E	F	I	G	H	T	E	R	N
A	Ό	A	Θ	P	H	A	R	C	H	I	T	E	C	T	A	Z
Σ	O	K	I	M	O	N	Y	T	Σ	A	D	I	H	I	M	Δ
H	E	P	Ю	N	N	Γ	L	H	Ю	P	F	F	C	A	H	H
T	Λ	Φ	S	I	Σ	A	H	R	Θ	F	I	I	A	I	X	Σ
Σ	Σ	E	Ί	Y	W	T	E	K	O	O	R	L	F	T	A	O
E	O	O	K	Y	C	H	S	E	I	T	Π	T	O	N	N	P
B	Λ	M	E	T	C	H	C	I	C	Δ	Ψ	O	O	T	I	T
Σ	A	R	O	A	P	I	I	E	T	Y	E	T	I	Σ	K	A
O	K	O	E	K	L	O	L	A	X	N	K	H	Γ	O	O	I
P	Σ	T	S	O	O	E	Λ	I	T	E	E	I	Ω	T	Σ	T
Y	A	C	P	Z	O	Σ	A	O	T	R	A	D	N	O	F	N
Π	Δ	O	X	N	Ύ	T	O	I	Γ	T	I	U	P	Λ	E	O
T	Θ	D	X	H	P	C	X	N	P	O	R	S	L	I	H	Δ
W	Ξ	Y	Λ	O	Y	P	Γ	O	Σ	S	Σ	D	T	Π	C	O
M	E	Φ	Σ	L	A	H	Σ	M	E	N	G	I	N	E	E	R

ACTOR	ΗΘΟΠΟΙΟΣ
ARCHITECT	ΑΡΧΙΤΕΚΤΟΝΑΣ
CARPENTER	ΞΥΛΟΥΡΓΟΣ
CHEF	ΣΕΦ
DENTIST	ΟΔΟΝΤΙΑΤΡΟΣ
DOCTOR	ΓΙΑΤΡΟΣ
ELECTRICIAN	ΗΛΕΚΤΡΟΛΟΓΟΣ
ENGINEER	ΜΗΧΑΝΙΚΟΣ
FIRE FIGHTER	ΠΥΡΟΣΒΕΣΤΗΣ
LAWYER	ΔΙΚΗΓΟΡΟΣ
NURSE	ΝΟΣΟΚΟΜΟΣ
PILOT	ΠΙΛΟΤΟΣ
POLICE OFFICER	ΑΣΤΥΝΟΜΙΚΟΣ
PSYCHIATRIST	ΨΥΧΙΑΤΡΟΣ
TEACHER	ΔΑΣΚΑΛΟΣ

PROFESSIONS 2

What did you want to be when you were growing up? Was it one of these professions?

```
Ύ I I R Σ S Я P A R A M E D I C B
Σ R O S S E F O R P E H A N E A T
H E O Ξ E T E L H T A H Ά I R S Δ
N B O L Γ S T I A T C T C B I I Θ
X M A Q I P S T P L C Φ E T A Ά O
E U U T Π A I I Σ X Ю R R Σ U A I
T L O S E T T C Σ H A A Ω A O B E
I P N I I S N I Σ H T Σ I Γ O Λ Π
Λ Ό N R Π C E A M H T H A M B A I
Λ D M O O N I N T H Λ Φ Λ Π O Ω Σ
A A O L Λ H C A Σ N X Ω A Θ H V T
K N Y F I Φ S Ψ N H U A Π P A Σ H
H C Σ H T Ω M M O K Ω O N O Π Θ M
X E I T I M E C H A N I C I Θ Ω O
I R K I K A Θ H Γ H T H Σ C K N N
Q Ό O X O P E Y T H Σ X X Ώ A O A
M N Σ P Σ O W Y Δ P A Y Λ I K O Σ
```

ACCOUNTANT	ΛΟΓΙΣΤΗΣ
ARTIST	ΚΑΛΛΙΤΕΧΝΗΣ
ATHLETE	ΑΘΛΗΤΗΣ
BARBER	ΚΟΜΜΩΤΗΣ
BUTCHER	ΧΑΣΑΠΗΣ
DANCER	ΧΟΡΕΥΤΗΣ
FLORIST	ΑΝΘΟΠΩΛΗΣ
MECHANIC	ΜΗΧΑΝΙΚΟΣ
MUSICIAN	ΜΟΥΣΙΚΟΣ
PARAMEDIC	ΔΙΑΣΩΣΤΗΣ
PLUMBER	ΥΔΡΑΥΛΙΚΟΣ
POLITICIAN	ΠΟΛΙΤΙΚΟΣ
PROFESSOR	ΚΑΘΗΓΗΤΗΣ
SCIENTIST	ΕΠΙΣΤΗΜΟΝΑΣ
TAILOR	ΡΑΦΤΗΣ

PROFESSIONS 3

There are thousands of unique and challenging careers out there to choose from. See if you can locate the following careers in the grid below.

```
L Σ E N M E T A Φ P A Σ T H Σ Θ T
Y Σ O P T A I N H T K A H H R V D
C O N I I Z H J A A X N Λ Ό E P R
B B I H O C Θ Γ O Y O Ω H T I H O
K Δ T E S Π P M Δ U Π Я E J R A T
R R H S P O O P F O R R Ω E R R A
E E Ψ M T O O K T I I N V W A M L
D N V H O M Φ A A N S I A E C A S
N E Σ I O Σ M Ω A M R H R L L C N
E D O Σ R H I R E D P E E E I I A
T R P A M D I O I Λ M A I R A S R
R A Y Σ P A S X Γ R Σ A Φ D M T T
A G O E N Ω A U A P X O G O L A E
B K Π D Д T A F B E A E Γ N H O N
E Λ H N A M P A Π M Ψ Φ Я H C R S
T Θ K I Ξ A T Σ O Γ H Δ O Ю Δ N T
Ψ A P A Σ H T Ω I T A P T Σ E O Π
```

BARTENDER	ΜΠΑΡΜΑΝ
BUS DRIVER	ΟΔΗΓΟΣ ΛΕΩΦΟΡΕΙΟΥ
FARMER	ΑΓΡΟΤΗΣ
FISHERMAN	ΨΑΡΑΣ
GARDENER	ΚΗΠΟΥΡΟΣ
JEWELER	ΚΟΣΜΗΜΑΤΟΠΩΛΗΣ
JOURNALIST	ΔΗΜΟΣΙΟΓΡΑΦΟΣ
MAIL CARRIER	ΤΑΧΥΔΡΟΜΟΣ
PHARMACIST	ΦΑΡΜΑΚΟΠΟΙΟΣ
SOLDIER	ΣΤΡΑΤΙΩΤΗΣ
TAXI DRIVER	ΟΔΗΓΟΣ ΤΑΞΙ
TRANSLATOR	ΜΕΤΑΦΡΑΣΤΗΣ
VETERINARIAN	ΚΤΗΝΙΑΤΡΟΣ

SOLAR SYSTEM

45

In 2015, the New Horizons spacecraft successfully completed the first flyby of dwarf planet Pluto. There is still so much to see and explore in our own solar system. Here are some key words from our celestial backyard.

```
T E L L I S T C R K E A T N Π
A Σ A T H Σ R Σ Σ O N A P Y O
Σ H Φ R H A A A M N I D S A Σ
H Δ M M T P H A M Φ H Δ A M E
T I P E H H Φ E Γ Γ A P I H I
H E R T K P O N O Σ F Ί L T Δ
M O A E O Π Λ O Y T Ω N A Σ Ω
O P O Δ T D Z S Д K A Ώ T Y N
K E I D M I E O B Y U T D Σ A
P T Ώ Δ V O P E T R H Λ I O Σ
H Σ I E S R O U A U Π E C K K
Ю A N Ί Ψ E H N J C L O R A Φ
Σ U N E P T U N E R M P Y I Ψ
S O L A R S Y S T E M E Γ Λ K
Ί N R U T A S T T M W A P H Σ
```

SOLAR SYSTEM	ΗΛΙΑΚΟ ΣΥΣΤΗΜΑ
MERCURY	ΕΡΜΗΣ
VENUS	ΑΦΡΟΔΙΤΗ
EARTH	ΓΗ
MOON	ΦΕΓΓΑΡΙ
MARS	ΑΡΗΣ
JUPITER	ΔΙΑΣ
SATURN	ΚΡΟΝΟΣ
URANUS	ΟΥΡΑΝΟΣ
NEPTUNE	ΠΟΣΕΙΔΩΝΑΣ
PLUTO	ΠΛΟΥΤΩΝΑΣ
SUN	ΗΛΙΟΣ
CRATER	ΚΡΑΤΗΡΑΣ
ASTEROID	ΑΣΤΕΡΟΕΙΔΗΣ
COMET	ΚΟΜΗΤΗΣ

MUSICAL INSTRUMENTS

Here are some musical instruments to get your foot tapping and your hands clapping.

Θ	H	S	X	T	H	A	O	Γ	Z	O	Λ	E	Σ	T
B	E	T	M	H	B	E	Σ	A	Ξ	O	Φ	Ω	N	O
O	T	N	T	U	A	P	N	M	Π	Y	Γ	Ώ	T	Y
G	U	I	T	A	R	R	A	O	Σ	P	C	N	E	M
O	L	L	P	A	M	D	M	A	B	Я	A	N	P	Π
K	F	O	H	I	R	B	P	O	S	M	O	T	M	A
K	H	I	A	X	A	M	O	A	N	I	O	B	U	E
I	N	V	O	K	O	N	X	U	D	I	A	R	R	Γ
Θ	Φ	A	I	N	O	O	O	R	R	G	C	Z	T	K
A	A	Λ	I	Ю	P	P	O	T	P	I	I	A	Σ	A
P	I	K	A	H	O	C	N	I	F	Φ	N	H	M	I
A	A	Γ	O	O	C	N	P	T	E	S	M	E	A	N
P	P	N	S	A	Y	E	A	T	E	Π	M	O	P	T
C	E	L	L	O	S	T	N	I	Λ	O	I	B	T	A
O	O	F	T	C	T	P	O	M	Π	O	N	I	N	I

ACCORDION
BAGPIPES
CELLO
DRUMS
FLUTE
GUITAR
HARMONICA
HARP
PIANO
SAXOPHONE
TAMBOURINE
TROMBONE
TRUMPET
TUBA
VIOLIN

AKOPNTEON
ΓKAINTA
TΣEΛO
NTPAMΣ
ΦΛAOYTO
KIΘAPA
ΦYΣAPMONIKA
APΠA
ΠIANO
ΣAΞOΦΩNO
NTEΦI
TPOMΠONI
TPOMΠETA
TOYMΠA
BIOΛI

EMOTIONS

This puzzle might make you happy, angry, or maybe even a little confused. See if you can complete this very emotional puzzle by finding all of the words in the grid.

I Ώ D Λ E Ξ W Ξ Θ Y M Ω M E N O Σ

Σ Ξ Σ U X I M C O N F U S E D O H

O O O U O A O Π Y Σ W A M I N X Φ

T E N I Σ R P P E A O B H E M Π O

K S A E S O P O N P A K M D E O B

H U Φ S M A N G Y R Δ H I Π R I I

Λ R H C H Σ R E R M T E E P E U Σ

Π P P O S Y A A M Σ E I M P Y Σ M

K R E N A N S I E Σ Σ N S E O E E

E I Π F M S B I Σ M A O O N N Ю N

N S A I E O P E E Y Ψ I E Σ U O O

E E I D R A X N T P O M Π A Λ O Σ

R D K E B C O O I Σ H Θ E O Ю K E

V A D N I Σ O S X Π A K N A P Ύ M

O S Z T A N H Σ Y X O Σ E E N T O

U D E R A C S Λ E A M H Θ Σ I A N

S D E I R R O W O X N O I T O M E

EMOTION	ΑΙΣΘΗΜΑ
HAPPY	ΧΑΡΟΥΜΕΝΟΣ
SAD	ΛΥΠΗΜΕΝΟΣ
EXCITED	ΕΝΘΟΥΣΙΑΣΜΕΝΟΣ
BORED	ΒΑΡΙΕΣΤΗΜΕΝΟΣ
SURPRISED	ΕΚΠΛΗΚΤΟΣ
SCARED	ΦΟΒΙΣΜΕΝΟΣ
ANGRY	ΘΥΜΩΜΕΝΟΣ
CONFUSED	ΜΠΕΡΔΕΜΕΝΟΣ
WORRIED	ΑΝΗΣΥΧΟΣ
NERVOUS	ΝΕΥΡΙΚΟΣ
PROUD	ΠΕΡΗΦΑΝΟΣ
CONFIDENT	ΠΕΠΕΙΣΜΕΝΟΣ
EMBARRASSED	ΝΤΡΟΠΙΑΣΜΕΝΟΣ
SHY	ΝΤΡΟΜΠΑΛΟΣ

ILLNESSES

If you are feeling any symptoms of the following conditions it might be time to visit the doctor. When you are feeling better the words below are waiting to be found.

S	Σ	O	T	E	P	Y	Π	Ά	E	X	G	A	R	C	C
A	Δ	O	E	H	C	A	D	A	E	H	I	A	I	O	D
I	I	N	Λ	X	C	T	N	K	E	Γ	S	N	L	U	Σ
Γ	I	M	H	A	N	R	O	O	O	H	F	D	L	G	C
P	P	I	O	A	Φ	R	A	Λ	S	E	R	F	D	H	N
E	K	R	Y	P	T	E	B	M	C	E	A	R	I	H	Ώ
Λ	O	T	E	S	P	O	K	T	P	L	B	C	A	B	Ώ
Λ	I	K	L	V	M	A	I	O	L	S	K	L	B	I	K
A	Γ	Δ	I	E	E	O	Γ	E	N	E	Ψ	E	E	A	D
I	A	I	N	Λ	N	F	R	I	N	O	B	Ξ	T	E	M
O	A	A	R	Θ	A	G	H	P	A	A	Π	A	E	S	D
P	P	B	D	Ό	Y	Φ	O	Π	R	Σ	B	N	S	U	O
P	G	H	T	B	M	X	E	Ύ	I	E	T	Θ	H	A	N
A	Д	T	A	M	Ω	Y	P	K	H	P	T	H	D	N	Ψ
I	L	H	Σ	N	Y	Λ	O	M	Γ	Ξ	Γ	M	N	Y	Δ
Δ	Ω	Σ	X	O	K	P	A	M	Π	E	Σ	A	X	H	B

ALLERGY	ΑΛΛΕΡΓΙΑ
CHICKENPOX	ΑΝΕΜΟΒΛΟΓΙΑ
COLD	ΚΡΥΩΜΑ
COUGH	ΒΗΧΑΣ
CRAMPS	ΚΡΑΜΠΕΣ
DIABETES	ΔΙΑΒΗΤΗΣ
DIARRHEA	ΔΙΑΡΡΟΙΑ
FEVER	ΠΥΡΕΤΟΣ
FLU	ΓΡΙΠΗ
HEADACHE	ΠΟΝΟΚΕΦΑΛΟΣ
INFECTION	ΜΟΛΥΝΣΗ
NAUSEA	ΝΑΥΤΙΑ
NOSEBLEED	ΑΙΜΟΡΡΑΓΙΑ ΣΤΗΝ μυτη
RASH	ΕΞΑΝΘΗΜΑ
STROKE	ΕΓΚΕΦΑΛΙΚΟ

ILLNESSES 2

Study these maladies so you can develop a healthy bilingual vocabulary.

M Ю Φ E U P W T Ί A R U K C B Θ

K A P Δ I A K H Π P O Σ B O Λ H

A X K C A T T A T R A E H Σ O A

M K A Ψ I M O R U X S Π O Ω M D

H A M N Ψ S P R A I N N E E I Ω

X I Γ P R C H Я U L O R P Π Ψ A

Y N A O Ψ U O R E Π U T V I O E

T A T C Y A B N O T Σ I Y Λ K Σ

A P A U S Λ I X C A R H S H A Я

O K K T A A A A I U Σ Φ P Ψ C Π

E I H H R M R Δ S I S Ί E I C S

M M X G O F Θ Y E M A S L A I M

A H I T E I Ω Σ H Σ Ю N I Λ D U

H M Σ X F M A P A Λ I Λ P O E M

M E Λ A N I A S E L S A E M N P

Γ S T A Δ E H C A H C A M O T S

ACCIDENT	ATYXHMA
ASTHMA	AΣΘMA
BRUISE	MEΛANIA
BURN	KAΨIMO
CONCUSSION	ΔIAΣEIΣH
CUT	KOΨIMO
EPILEPSY	EΠIΛHΨIA
FRACTURE	KATAΓMA
HEART ATTACK	KAPΔIAKH ΠPOΣBOΛH
MEASLES	IΛAPA
MIGRAINE	HMIKPANIA
MUMPS	MAΓOYΛAΔEΣ
SPRAIN	ΔIAΣTPEMA
STOMACH ACHE	ΣTOMAXOΠONOΣ
VIRUS	IΩΣH

QUESTIONS

50

Here are some basic questions and terms that you might hear frequently used in any language. Why? Because. Find these questionable terms and phrases below.

O	Ψ	R	K	Ξ	N	R	A	B	Я	E	R	E	H	W
E	T	E	Σ	H	Θ	H	O	B	E	M	A	N	R	H
I	Ό	I	N	S	A	T	M	N	O	Ό	I	W	Ω	A
E	S	H	Ω	Ύ	Φ	Σ	N	Γ	Π	A	P	T	Γ	T
M	X	O	C	P	Λ	O	Δ	O	Ω	N	K	I	P	T
P	N	E	H	L	A	O	T	L	Σ	N	A	B	Ώ	I
L	Ω	Ю	H	Δ	I	E	Π	E	E	T	M	Π	F	M
E	S	U	A	C	E	B	Ί	O	I	B	O	Ω	M	E
H	H	O	W	M	U	C	H	N	Σ	Σ	Σ	Σ	A	I
U	O	Y	E	R	A	W	O	H	A	O	O	N	F	S
O	W	W	Π	E	A	T	E	Π	I	I	Π	I	Ί	I
Y	M	Ξ	O	T	Φ	F	O	I	E	G	N	Ύ	O	T
N	A	I	N	H	Y	Λ	W	Y	M	E	Ώ	K	A	Π
A	N	X	X	F	Λ	T	H	O	H	T	I	T	O	N
C	Y	E	C	A	T	W	O	W	H	A	T	Y	Ώ	I

BECAUSE	ΕΠΕΙΔΗ
HOW	ΠΩΣ
HOW ARE YOU	ΠΩΣ ΕΙΣΑΙ
HOW FAR	ΠΟΣΟ ΜΑΚΡΙΑ
HOW MANY	ΠΟΣΑ ΠΟΛΛΑ
HOW MUCH	ΠΟΣΟ ΠΟΛΎ
CAN YOU HELP ME	μπορειτε ΝΑ ΜΕ ΒΟΗΘΗΣΕΤΕ
WHAT	ΤΙ
WHAT TIME IS IT	ΤΙ ΩΡΑ ΕΊΝΑΙ
WHEN	ΠΟΤΕ
WHERE	ΠΟΥ
WHO	ΠΟΙΟΣ
WHY	ΓΙΑΤΙ

AT A RESTAURANT

Table for two? Welcome to our Learn with Word Search restaurant. On the menu are the following helpful and delicious restaurant related words. Enjoy!

```
D L A T S I L E N I W R M E N O Y
Д Я I Ά Σ T H E B I L L H Λ T T A
Θ I Σ B C E B P A Δ I N O M O A T
V A A K Ώ Δ T Д X D Y Γ E N Y I R
E O P O N D B E Ώ L A N K H A Π E
O W K N I P I Φ Σ P U Я Ψ Σ Λ Σ S
M A E I I E C N I T A N O A E Ω S
E I M Ω T R A A N Λ E P C Π T I E
Σ T Σ P Ю K Σ P Σ E O Π I H E P D
H E O Π S M E Φ P T R Δ O K Σ Y A
M R Γ N O N Я P I E O Δ Ω T C K O
E T O Σ T Ω I B O P T N P P P K Π
P E Λ A Ω H P K Π I I I T Σ H A N
I Ξ A P G E N I P Π A I Z H Д M X
A T T S Σ I O T S A F K A E R B A
N X A Ξ R Y A M A I N C O U R S E
O I K D R E S T R O O M S Ώ Δ F Φ
```

APPETIZER	ΟΡΕΚΤΙΚΟ
BREAKFAST	ΠΡΩΙΝΟ
DESSERT	ΕΠΙΔΟΡΠΙΟ
DINNER	ΒΡΑΔΙΝΟ
DRINK	ΠΙΝΩ
EAT	ΤΡΩΩ
LUNCH	ΜΕΣΗΜΕΡΙΑΝΟ
MAIN COURSE	ΚΥΡΙΩΣ ΠΙΑΤΟ
MENU	ΜΕΝΟΥ
NAPKINS	ΧΑΡΤΟΠΕΤΣΕΤΕΣ
RESTROOMS	ΤΟΥΑΛΕΤΕΣ
THE BILL	ΛΟΓΑΡΙΑΣΜΟΣ
TIP	ΦΙΛΟΔΩΡΗΜΑ
WAITER	ΣΕΡΒΙΤΟΡΟΣ
WINE LIST	ΚΑΤΑΛΟΓΟΣ ΜΕ ΚΡΑΣΙΑ

AT THE HOTEL

After that delicious meal it is time to head back to the hotel and relax. Here is a list of hotel words that might help give you a good night's sleep.

```
Γ Y M N Α Σ T H P I O H N P P T S
Y E O T E L E V I S I O N O O D B
Π B W I Y N T C E T I T T W M D L
O R R S T Ύ O O O I T Д E E X Y U O
Δ I E U C A K H P V T L A E G T E
O H P O T I M E P H R P K G A T Ά
X I A I T S C Ω Λ E T E A O I E X
H Σ P E N E I E Δ I L G S E F O I
K E T X R T Φ D T A E E Λ M Π E N
O Y E O I Ω E O T A I X T E O R T
Y E L Δ N T Y P I O O Σ T Ю L O E
B K I O Ω A A K N N N Σ E M O O R
E Σ O N Λ A Λ B E E E E O S P J F N
P O T E Ψ E Ύ N E T T D D T H E E
T Π T Ξ I E H Σ A P O E Λ H T Π T
E A E Δ Ω M A T I O K A Y L T E Y
Σ N I H Φ S T E K N A L B E D Ύ I
```

BED	KPEBATI
BLANKETS	KOYBEPTEΣ
DO NOT DISTURB	MHN ENOXΛEITE
GYM	ΓYMNAΣTHPIO
HOTEL	ΞENOΔOXEIO
INTERNET	INTEPNET
KEY	KΛEIΔI
LUGGAGE	AΠOΣKEYEΣ
RECEPTION	YΠOΔOXH
ROOM	ΔΩMATIO
ROOM SERVICE	YΠHPEΣIA ΔΩMATIOY
TELEPHONE	THΛEΦΩNO
TELEVISION	THΛEOPAΣH
TOILET PAPER	XAPTI TOYAΛETAΣ
TOWEL	ΠETΣETA

SUBJECTS

53

Were you a good student? Here are some subjects that you may have studied long ago, or may be learning right now. Study these challenging subject translations.

Ω	E	X	I	Σ	T	O	P	I	A	Δ	C	I	S	U	M	E
E	E	T	S	E	G	A	U	G	N	A	L	S	S	O	D	O
H	A	E	E	T	T	E	C	N	E	I	C	S	E	H	E	Ω
Z	I	I	E	C	O	N	O	M	I	C	S	Π	N	N	L	R
L	Φ	K	N	N	P	M	K	G	M	U	I	T	I	F	Y	M
Γ	O	A	N	E	G	I	G	A	R	X	R	C	S	C	Ώ	H
E	Σ	Σ	I	A	C	I	Θ	X	E	A	I	Ψ	U	E	P	X
Ω	O	T	E	E	T	H	N	I	T	D	P	H	B	H	H	A
Γ	Λ	I	N	M	M	Y	P	E	E	M	K	H	I	I	O	N
P	I	K	K	A	H	H	R	M	E	I	Z	L	Y	S	Γ	I
A	Φ	A	T	O	Σ	T	X	T	Σ	R	O	Θ	C	T	Λ	K
Φ	Ψ	I	T	E	N	P	Σ	Y	S	S	I	I	Π	O	Ω	H
I	K	A	I	P	Ά	O	O	I	O	I	S	N	Ύ	R	Σ	K
A	Ω	Σ	H	H	I	M	M	P	Π	Y	M	A	G	Y	Σ	I
O	O	A	W	M	I	K	H	I	H	E	Ψ	E	T	Д	E	Σ
B	I	O	L	O	G	Y	H	P	K	M	A	T	H	X	Σ	Y
P	L	K	B	I	O	Λ	O	Γ	I	A	E	F	M	C	Я	Φ

ART	ΕΙΚΑΣΤΙΚΑ
BIOLOGY	ΒΙΟΛΟΓΙΑ
BUSINESS	ΕΠΙΧΕΙΡΗΣΕΙΣ
CHEMISTRY	ΧΗΜΕΙΑ
ECONOMICS	ΟΙΚΟΝΟΜΙΚΑ
ENGINEERING	ΜΗΧΑΝΙΚΗ
GEOGRAPHY	ΓΕΩΓΡΑΦΙΑ
HISTORY	ΙΣΤΟΡΙΑ
LANGUAGES	ΓΛΩΣΣΕΣ
MATH	ΜΑΘΗΜΑΤΙΚΑ
MEDICINE	ΙΑΤΡΙΚΗ
MUSIC	ΜΟΥΣΙΚΗ
PHILOSOPHY	ΦΙΛΟΣΟΦΙΑ
PHYSICS	ΦΥΣΙΚΗ
SCIENCE	ΕΠΙΣΤΗΜΕΣ

MATH

Math. Some people love it, and some people hate it. Add these words to your vocabulary and multiply your language skills.

```
Η Σ Ε Θ Σ Ο Ρ Π Γ Ο Τ Σ Ο Σ Ο Π Π
Σ Ο D Ι Θ C Γ Η Γ Ε Μ Β Α Δ Ο Ν Α
Ε Τ Β Ε Κ R Ι Κ Σ Σ Ω Ο Α Λ Ι R Ρ
Ρ Ε L Μ Ε Α Ο Τ Α Ε Ν Μ Λ V Α Χ Α
Ι Θ Ε U U Σ Ρ Κ Ε Ο Ρ Α Ε L Ο Π Λ
Α Α L L G L Α Ε Ι Μ Π Ι U Τ Ν Α Λ
Ι Κ L Ο Η Ρ Τ Τ Τ Λ Η C Α Γ Ρ Ρ Η
Δ Υ Α V Α Σ C Ι Α Υ Ι Τ R Φ Α Ι Λ
D Ν R Χ Ν Α Ω Σ Ρ D Ο Ο Ι Μ Α Θ Α
D Ι Α Τ R R Ι Σ Ν L Τ Ι Σ R Д Μ Ε
Ι S Ρ Τ Ε Α Ύ Ε Ι Α Ι Α Π Ο Α Η Q
V D Β L Σ Μ Ρ Ν L Ξ Λ C Ζ Μ S Τ U
Ι U U Μ Ο R Ο U Π Κ Ε Α Α Μ Ο Ι Α
S R Ο Ρ Ε R C Ε Ν Τ Α G Ε Τ Η Κ Τ
Ι Σ Ξ Ρ Γ L Α Ι G Ε Ι Ν Ύ R Ι Η Ι
Ο Α Η L Α D D Ι Τ Ι Ο Ν Ο Д Α Ο Ο
Ν Ι Ρ C L Q Ά Д L F R Α C Τ Ι Ο Ν
```

ADDITION	ΠΡΟΣΘΕΣΗ
AREA	ΕΜΒΑΔΟΝ
ARITHMETIC	ΑΡΙΘΜΗΤΙΚΗ
CALCULATOR	ΚΟΜΠΙΟΥΤΕΡΑΚΙ
DIVISION	ΔΙΑΙΡΕΣΗ
EQUATION	ΕΞΙΣΩΣΗ
FRACTION	ΚΛΑΣΜΑ
GEOMETRY	ΓΕΩΜΕΤΡΙΑ
MULTIPLICATION	ΠΟΛΛΑΠΛΑΣΙΑΣΜΟΣ
PARALLEL	ΠΑΡΑΛΛΗΛΑ
PERCENTAGE	ΠΟΣΟΣΤΟ
PERPENDICULAR	ΚΑΘΕΤΟΣ
RULER	ΧΑΡΑΚΑΣ
SUBTRACTION	ΑΦΑΙΡΕΣΗ
VOLUME	ΟΓΚΟΣ

AT THE AIRPORT

It is estimated that globally there are over 100,000 flights per day. Here are some common airport related terms for you to learn while they try to find your lost baggage.

Ο Δ Ι Ε Θ Ν Η Σ Ω Ι Ε Γ Ο Π Α Ρ Σ

T E R M I N A L O B C I Π Ю O O E

Σ Ο Ε Σ Η R Β Α Ν Ι Μ Ι S Y Μ Ι Σ

Α Ε Ι Σ Ι Τ Η Ρ Ι Ο Ρ Ε Φ Θ Λ Ρ Τ

Α Α Η Ι Ξ Ε Β Ζ Ρ Ε R Ω Α Α Σ Η Ι

Τ Ι Ε Ν Ν Α Σ Δ Ώ U Λ Τ Χ Ο Δ Τ Λ

C Η Γ Ρ G Τ Ο Η Τ Ι Σ Α Μ Γ Ε Α Α

Ι Σ Τ G Ο Ρ Ε R Ρ Σ Τ Ο Φ Λ Ε Β Β

Τ R Α Α Ε Σ Α R Ο Ω Ρ Ι Ω Σ Ρ Α Σ

S G Κ Α Ί Ρ Κ Κ Ν Δ Χ Ν C Α Α Ι Υ

Ε Μ Ε Ε Ε Υ Ι Α Α Α Ε Α S Κ Ε Δ Τ

Μ Α Ο D Ό Τ Α Ι Φ Ι Τ S Ν Ξ Ε W Ι

Ο Ν F Τ Α Η Δ W Ο Ο Ρ Ι Ι Α Τ Τ R

D Η F Μ S Ο Ί Χ Ν Ο Σ Φ Ο Τ Α Ο U

F Ε Ρ Я Ρ U Η L R U Α S C Ν G Φ C

Ώ Ε Ν Ε Α W C Τ F Α R C R Ι Α Χ Ε

Τ Β Α Τ R Ο Ρ R Ι Α R R Ι V Α L S

AIRCRAFT	ΑΕΡΟΣΚΑΦΟΣ
AIRPORT	ΑΕΡΟΔΡΟΜΙΟ
ARRIVALS	ΑΦΙΞΕΙΣ
BAGGAGE	ΒΑΛΙΤΣΕΣ
CUSTOMS	ΤΕΛΩΝΕΙΟ
DEPARTURES	ΑΝΑΧΩΡΗΣΕΙΣ
DOMESTIC	ΕΓΧΩΡΙΟΣ
GATE	ΠΥΛΗ
INTERNATIONAL	ΔΙΕΘΝΗΣ
PASSPORT	ΔΙΑΒΑΤΗΡΙΟ
RUNWAY	ΑΕΡΟΔΙΑΔΡΟΜΟΣ
SECURITY	ΑΣΦΑΛΕΙΑ
TAKEOFF	ΑΠΟΓΕΙΩΣΗ
TERMINAL	ΤΕΡΜΑΤΙΚΟΣ ΣΤΑΘΜΟΣ
TICKET	ΕΙΣΙΤΗΡΙΟ

ON THE FARM

56

Farming has existed since 10,000 BC. If you work on a farm, or just like eating food, here are a some farm words for you harvest.

Ρ Ώ Υ R Φ Ε Ο Ρ Τ D Τ Ι Σ Σ Γ
Ν Κ Ί Η Χ Θ Η R Ο Ο Π Α Π Ι Α
Ω Ό Η Ε Ε Ρ Α Ν R Λ Δ Μ Α Χ Λ
N W C H I C K E N Y K L P B O
W O K Ό T E T M S O Γ A T T Π
Π C Σ O Y S P H K Π O X A Φ O
F L R O O Z E O Я O Y Y Λ Σ Y
A A D O P E P Y E T P O O R Λ
D M R L P A Π Θ C O O L Γ I A
D B L M Σ S Δ P Σ K Y T O Γ Δ
T U R K E Y E I O C N O E Ψ I
B T C S M R T Z A B I Λ Λ Ύ Γ
Δ A R K Σ H T O P Γ A P N I T
Θ O E H Γ K H E Ά Δ E T H O Ύ
H G I P P E T K A P T H O O O

BULL	ΤΑΥΡΟΣ
CHICKEN	ΚΟΤΟΠΟΥΛΟ
COW	ΑΓΕΛΑΔΑ
CROPS	ΣΠΑΡΤΑ
DONKEY	ΓΑΙΔΑΡΟΣ
DUCK	ΠΑΠΙΑ
FARMER	ΑΓΡΟΤΗΣ
GOAT	ΓΙΔΑ
HORSE	ΑΛΟΓΟ
LAMB	ΑΡΝΙ
PIG	ΓΟΥΡΟΥΝΙ
ROOSTER	ΚΟΚΟΡΑΣ
SHEEP	ΠΡΟΒΑΤΟ
TRACTOR	ΤΡΑΚΤΕΡ
TURKEY	ΓΑΛΟΠΟΥΛΑ

SIGHTSEEING

Time to get out there and experience all there is to see. How do you prefer to explore a new city? Try exploring these highly rated sightseeing words.

H M O Y Σ E I O S R I N E V U O S

E N Ώ H I N Y R E L L A G T R A Ό

Ξ H A P E A O D U A P E Π Ά D P I

S M Ю X P E R I R I Σ V A S I A Ξ

Y E H E H O M E T E N A P E R R E

E I M Σ C M M U I A T S K M E K N

L A M M O A H P S T M Θ O D C O A

K P A O C K O K R E E R I Ά T O Γ

B C I T N Φ I A I Σ U U O S I B O

E M O N O U C T H Φ G M I F O E Σ

P N H P E T M T Ω R A R A A N D I

E R H E I B E E U I U P A P S I Γ

I Λ M O T X Y O N O Δ O Γ Y E U N

Π T N W N D T O T T P I O O H G O

I S Σ H T P A X Σ C S Ά Ξ E T M U

A N Σ S J A Ξ I O Θ E A T A H Ω T

O Δ H Γ Ί E Σ A T Σ I P Y O T B Φ

ART GALLERY	ΕΚΘΕΣΗ ΤΕΧΝΗΣ
ATTRACTIONS	ΑΞΙΟΘΕΑΤΑ
CAMCORDER	ΚΑΜΕΡΑ
CAMERA	ΦΩΤΟΓΡΑΦΙΚΗ ΜΗΧΑΝΗ
DIRECTIONS	ΟΔΗΓΊΕΣ
GUIDE BOOK	ΤΑΞΙΔΙΩΤΙΚΟΣ οδηγοσ
INFORMATION	ΠΛΗΡΟΦΟΡΙΕΣ
MAP	ΧΑΡΤΗΣ
MONUMENTS	ΜΝΗΜΕΙΑ
MUSEUM	ΜΟΥΣΕΙΟ
PARK	ΠΑΡΚΟ
RUINS	ΕΡΕΙΠΙΑ
SOUVENIRS	ΣΟΥΒΕΝΙΡ
TOUR GUIDE	ΞΕΝΑΓΟΣ
TOURIST	ΤΟΥΡΙΣΤΑΣ

AT THE BEACH

Time to hit the beach for some sun, sand and surf. Below you will find a list of warm beach related words.

S A N D C A S T L E Λ Ώ Ά Φ O O
A E Σ S E A A G V O E A T E C M
A N S O H B N P N Π L Y K K E M
Y A T S M O D P A I A Σ O Θ A A
O Y Ψ I A M V P F P M Y P A N Ό
I A T Δ H L A E A Θ B M T A Ί Π
Λ Γ O E A Λ G K L A A A I S E A
H O Λ T I U I N Δ S M Λ K W A O
A Σ A A A S G A U Y A K A E S P
I Ω O R L B K N K S Σ N Π Σ E T
Λ Σ D I P I S E I O S I E W Σ Σ
A T T E K C U B N F Σ Ί Λ A E A
Y H R A R E E A E O R N O V P K
Γ Σ N E H A E Ά I I F U U E Φ Z
E A E H C K O Λ Y M Π I S S O H
Θ N H H Ω T H N E S Π Ώ X E S H

BEACH	ΠΑΡΑΛΙΑ
BUCKET	ΚΟΥΒΑΔΑΚΙ
HAT	ΚΑΠΕΛΟ
LIFE GUARD	ΝΑΥΑΓΟΣΩΣΤΗΣ
OCEAN	ΩΚΕΑΝΟΣ
SAND	ΑΜΜΟΣ
SANDCASTLE	ΚΑΣΤΡΟ ΑΠΌ ΑΜΜΟ
SEA	ΘΑΛΑΣΣΑ
SHOVEL	ΦΤΥΑΡΑΚΙ
SUN	ΗΛΙΟΣ
SUNGLASSES	ΓΥΑΛΙΑ ΗΛΙΟΥ
SUNSCREEN	ΑΝΤΙΗΛΙΑΚΟ
SURFING	ΣΕΡΦ
SWIMMING	ΚΟΛΥΜΠΙ
WAVES	ΚΥΜΑΤΑ

OPPOSITES 1

Is the museum near or far? Is it expensive to get in or not? Start studying these opposite terms, and you may find out.

Η Σ Ο Λ Α Γ Ε Μ Α Λ Α Κ Ο Σ Η
Ρ Α Ο Ω Υ Σ D W Π Σ Ν Ю Ώ Χ Σ
Α Ψ Η Λ Ο Σ Α Τ Σ Λ Κ Α Κ Ο Σ
Τ Μ Ю Ρ Η Ε Μ Κ Ο Τ Α Α Σ Ύ Κ
Ν Η Γ Κ Ε Ψ Τ Υ Λ Τ Ε Τ Ζ Η Λ
Β Υ Η Ε Σ F Υ Α Α Ε D Γ Υ Τ Η
L Τ Ο Κ Ε Τ Α Η Κ Α D Τ Ν Σ Ρ
Τ Ζ Φ Α Ο Ρ G Ι Β D Ά Ι Ο Ο Ο
Η G Χ Τ Β Ν S G Ο Ο D Ν W Λ Σ
Β Τ Ί D Ι Σ Τ Η Ρ W Ε Ο Ε Η Ο
Ψ Ε Υ Υ Δ D L Ο Ο Τ R Ρ Τ Μ Ρ
Η Α Η R Τ S L L Σ R Ν Δ Η Α Κ
Ε S S Τ D R Α Η Α Α Τ Β Ε Χ Ι
R Ι G S Ο F Τ Ν Ε Μ Χ Ε Θ Ε Μ
Ε Α Η Τ Д Ό Α Ρ Τ Ν S V Β V Η

BIG	ΜΕΓΑΛΟΣ
SMALL	ΜΙΚΡΟΣ
WIDE	ΠΛΑΤΥΣ
NARROW	ΣΤΕΝΟΣ
TALL	ΨΗΛΟΣ
SHORT	ΚΟΝΤΟΣ
HIGH	ΥΨΗΛΟΣ
LOW	ΧΑΜΗΛΟΣ
GOOD	ΚΑΛΟΣ
BAD	ΚΑΚΟΣ
WET	ΥΓΡΟΣ
DRY	ΣΤΕΓΝΟΣ
HARD	ΣΚΛΗΡΟΣ
SOFT	ΜΑΛΑΚΟΣ

OPPOSITES 2

Would you be opposed or in favor of some more opposite words? For better or worse, here are some more words to study and find.

A	I	E	A	A	E	Ό	K	A	Θ	A	P	O	Σ	G
S	A	Θ	T	H	H	T	K	N	Ψ	C	Ю	O	O	O
P	Я	M	Y	A	Ω	T	P	O	H	P	Θ	Z	T	Γ
M	U	Q	T	S	A	F	Y	I	K	A	Σ	R	Σ	P
N	I	W	U	P	I	N	O	X	Λ	L	O	Λ	E	H
O	E	H	O	I	C	O	Σ	T	Σ	O	X	Φ	Z	Γ
U	E	P	C	L	E	A	N	O	A	Ω	Y	N	H	O
R	X	T	O	W	S	T	B	Σ	T	P	Σ	X	N	P
S	P	S	R	P	O	I	C	O	O	Σ	H	T	E	O
I	E	O	R	H	P	P	D	K	Ί	N	I	T	O	Σ
D	N	Π	Ό	K	A	I	L	I	C	Δ	H	E	Ύ	Σ
G	S	T	A	E	R	X	O	M	T	P	Ώ	T	Λ	X
R	I	G	H	T	A	I	C	Ω	B	Z	T	Ξ	Φ	K
T	V	C	Y	H	Σ	O	Γ	P	A	I	A	Δ	A	G
H	E	U	O	Θ	O	P	Y	B	Ω	Δ	H	Σ	N	I

FAST	ΓΡΗΓΟΡΟΣ
SLOW	ΑΡΓΟΣ
RIGHT	ΣΩΣΤΟΣ
WRONG	ΛΑΘΟΣ
CLEAN	ΚΑΘΑΡΟΣ
DIRTY	ΒΡΩΜΙΚΟΣ
QUIET	ΗΣΥΧΟΣ
NOISY	ΘΟΡΥΒΩΔΗΣ
EXPENSIVE	ΑΚΡΙΒΟΣ
CHEAP	ΦΤΗΝΟΣ
HOT	ΖΕΣΤΟΣ
COLD	ΚΡΥΟΣ
OPEN	ΑΝΟΙΧΤΟΣ
CLOSED	ΚΛΕΙΣΤΟΣ

OPPOSITES 3

They say that opposites attract. See if you are attracted to the list of opposite words below. Find them in the grid, or don't.

B E G I N N I N G N O R T S K
W E A K H Φ I T A F E O H A R
Ό Φ N S U H H H I Δ U W G D A
F Ω H D Y S Γ N T X E L I O D
K T E Ξ Σ E Ί H W A J I L B I
H E O O M A O A H E F D O Φ F
Я I E A E Σ Δ Y Σ K O Λ O Σ F
I N T B S O A P O O Φ B E O I
I O O X N T I L M I Y D M N C
Σ Σ O G L Π Ω Λ A A A C P I U
E T M E Ά E E A N V Я H T E L
H E E Σ O Λ O K Y E X A Y T T
E E H Λ Z B Λ N Δ P F Ί O O K
Π A Λ I O Σ O T A N Y Δ E K K
O K F Y E Σ Y X O N T P O Σ P

FULL
EMPTY
NEW
OLD
LIGHT
DARK
EASY
DIFFICULT
STRONG
WEAK
FAT
THIN
BEGINNING
END

ΓΕΜΑΤΟΣ
ΑΔΕΙΟΣ
ΝΕΟΣ
ΠΑΛΙΟΣ
ΦΩΤΕΙΝΟΣ
ΣΚΟΤΕΙΝΟΣ
ΕΥΚΟΛΟΣ
ΔΥΣΚΟΛΟΣ
ΔΥΝΑΤΟΣ
ΑΔΥΝΑΜΟΣ
ΧΟΝΤΡΟΣ
ΛΕΠΤΟΣ
ΑΡΧΗ
ΤΕΛΟΣ

OPPOSITES 4

An antonym is a word opposite in meaning to another. A synonym is a word that has the same or similar meaning to another word. Find the antonyms from the word list in the puzzle grid.

G Λ A Ά E Z C I Z M Γ Λ O A Ό
N H K H Z E D F K M E E T K P
S Y D M U I Λ Ό Ύ I Ψ Σ Φ W I
Λ A Д E X R M Я H M E T A R Ί
M I Y Z E G Π N E N A P Γ A Я
H T N T E Ί P Λ E N K K E Π Σ
Σ K A S E H Γ Я K A T X P P O
C A O Σ I E T M F S R Ω D I I
O W M O W D B T R R T P T N A
X I Λ C P A E I Θ O T I Ώ T T
Ю T T X R R F R Σ S I Σ N Δ Y
D H E R E S O W A A E O Ω Ξ E
M O C H E A R L Y F K M P P Λ
O U T S I D E T A L E Σ I D E
H T I W N T A H V T E A Σ Ύ T

NEAR	ΚΟΝΤΑ
FAR	ΜΑΚΡΙΑ
HERE	ΕΔΩ
THERE	ΕΚΕΙ
WITH	ΜΕ
WITHOUT	ΧΩΡΙΣ
BEFORE	ΠΡΙΝ
AFTER	ΜΕΤΑ
EARLY	ΝΩΡΙΣ
LATE	ΑΡΓΑ
INSIDE	ΜΕΣΑ
OUTSIDE	ΕΞΩ
FIRST	ΠΡΩΤΟΣ
LAST	ΤΕΛΕΥΤΑΙΟΣ

MATERIALS

63

We encounter many different materials on a daily basis. Some are strong enough to hold up buildings and others are soft and flexible. Here is a list of common materials to choose from as we continue to build your language skills.

Λ	J	X	E	T	C	Ψ	Ύ	I	L	Д	Φ	A	Ά	T
E	Σ	Ά	Γ	Y	Ψ	O	Σ	E	A	E	C	E	G	K
Y	P	M	Π	E	T	O	N	O	O	I	E	L	L	P
K	L	R	X	S	K	K	S	A	Σ	Λ	E	T	A	O
O	A	A	E	Λ	H	I	Ω	I	I	Y	Y	I	S	Y
X	T	L	A	C	R	T	S	T	L	Λ	P	Ξ	S	Π
P	I	X	Γ	O	R	Σ	N	A	I	V	A	X	Σ	E
Y	N	E	Y	Λ	H	A	A	K	N	Σ	E	Σ	R	T
Σ	U	T	A	Λ	M	Λ	O	M	H	D	M	R	T	P
O	M	Ω	Λ	A	Ю	Π	E	M	I	S	E	D	Ю	A
Σ	T	U	I	T	A	A	I	A	X	P	T	O	I	E
I	N	Δ	Ύ	E	O	O	M	D	P	A	A	O	S	R
O	Σ	O	M	M	A	O	L	O	Я	C	L	W	N	T
E	T	E	R	C	N	O	C	I	T	S	A	L	P	E
S	H	Y	H	D	G	M	A	T	E	R	I	A	L	T

CLAY	ΓΥΨΟΣ
CONCRETE	ΜΠΕΤΟΝ
COPPER	ΧΑΛΚΟΣ
DIAMOND	ΔΙΑΜΑΝΤΙ
GLASS	ΓΥΑΛΙ
GOLD	ΧΡΥΣΟΣ
MATERIAL	ΥΛΙΚΟ
METAL	ΜΕΤΑΛΛΟ
PLASTIC	ΠΛΑΣΤΙΚΟ
PLATINUM	ΛΕΥΚΟΧΡΥΣΟΣ
SAND	ΑΜΜΟΣ
SILVER	ΑΣΗΜΙ
STEEL	ΑΤΣΑΛΙ
STONE	ΠΕΤΡΑ
WOOD	ΞΥΛΟ

MATERIALS 2

See if you can handle another shipment of common materials. Be sure to handle each one with care.

B T C I M A R E C O P A M P A M

Z A T I R O N E A Ψ R A E Ω N Σ

K C I R B Ά Λ K P Σ I Δ E P O O

O M T R A A R Y E A M Θ Θ Z Ξ I

L E A T H E R Π B P P Λ T Ψ E N

E S N T B I Ί F R Δ A Y Ξ O I I

S T I B P A C T R Σ O M T X Δ M

Ω I U D A E S B T P A Σ I I Ω Y

S R M A M O K I Π B I K T K T O

T N U E I E X M I M A P A T O Λ

O O N L P O M Ω E B A A N M A A

T T I B A Ω T N M X Ώ J I A T H

B T M R R K O A E A Y W O Φ Σ Ω

S O U A O A B M O Σ Δ E P M A Z

B C L M I E Y N O M T O Y B Λ O

S T A I N L E S S S T E E L I A

ALUMINUM	ΑΛΟΥΜΙΝΙΟ
BRASS	ΜΠΡΟΥΤΖΟΣ
BRICK	ΤΟΥΒΛΟ
CEMENT	ΤΣΙΜΕΝΟ
CERAMIC	ΚΕΡΑΜΙΚΟ
COTTON	ΒΑΜΒΑΚΙ
IRON	ΣΙΔΕΡΟ
LEAD	ΜΟΛΥΒΔΟΣ
LEATHER	ΔΕΡΜΑ
MARBLE	ΜΑΡΜΑΡΟ
PAPER	ΧΑΡΤΙ
RUBBER	ΛΑΣΤΙΧΟ
SOIL	ΧΩΜΑ
STAINLESS STEEL	ΑΝΟΞΕΙΔΩΤΟ ΑΤΣΑΛΙ
TITANIUM	ΤΙΤΑΝΙΟ

SOMETHING TO DRINK?

We've made it through the first half of the book. Time to stop and have something to drink. Can we suggest one of the following?

I	Σ	A	P	K	O	N	I	K	K	O	K	O	Γ	Ю
T	O	N	I	Σ	T	Y	O	Π	A	K	T	O	B	B
T	Ό	Λ	Σ	N	E	T	Π	H	W	A	T	E	R	E
N	J	Γ	A	Λ	A	Φ	Z	K	P	Ά	I	A	E	E
Д	E	E	P	T	M	Π	A	I	I	T	N	E	D	R
A	Я	P	K	Ξ	N	Σ	M	K	N	D	V	T	W	H
T	O	Δ	O	T	O	Y	C	A	Y	E	O	A	I	E
O	E	O	K	M	O	E	P	X	Σ	R	D	Ξ	N	E
H	S	H	Y	P	W	Π	I	R	I	Ξ	K	G	E	F
H	Y	X	E	I	M	H	G	O	R	J	A	M	R	F
A	Σ	T	Λ	Π	Σ	M	I	L	K	P	U	H	C	O
N	V	B	Y	R	J	K	N	S	M	R	B	I	A	C
W	E	P	L	P	Θ	Ξ	I	A	K	Ά	E	Θ	C	Φ
I	A	Σ	T	O	Θ	W	H	I	T	E	W	I	N	E
H	C	A	P	P	U	C	C	I	N	O	Y	O	A	H

BEER	ΜΠΥΡΑ
BRANDY	ΜΠΡΑΝΤΙ
CAPPUCCINO	ΚΑΠΟΥΤΣΙΝΟ
CHAMPAGNE	ΣΑΜΠΑΝΙΑ
COFFEE	ΚΑΦΕΣ
GIN	ΤΖΙΝ
JUICE	ΧΥΜΟΣ
MILK	ΓΑΛΑ
RED WINE	ΚΟΚΚΙΝΟ ΚΡΑΣΙ
RUM	ΡΟΥΜΙ
TEA	ΤΣΑΙ
VODKA	ΒΟΤΚΑ
WATER	ΝΕΡΟ
WHISKEY	ΟΥΙΣΚΙ
WHITE WINE	ΛΕΥΚΟ ΚΡΑΣΙ

REVIEW: NUMBERS

66

Review Jumble: The translations in the word list below have been scrambled. Draw lines between the left and right columns to find the correct translations.

ONE	ENA
TWO	ΔΕΚΑΤΕΣΣΕΡΑ
THREE	ΤΕΣΣΕΡΑ
FOUR	ΕΞΙ
FIVE	ΔΥΟ
SIX	ΕΝΝΙΑ
SEVEN	ΕΝΤΕΚΑ
EIGHT	ΕΦΤΑ
NINE	ΔΩΔΕΚΑ
TEN	ΔΕΚΑΠΕΝΤΕ
ELEVEN	ΤΡΙΑ
TWELVE	ΔΕΚΑ
THIRTEEN	ΠΕΝΤΕ
FOURTEEN	ΔΕΚΑΤΡΙΑ
FIFTEEN	ΟΧΤΩ

REVIEW: MORE NUMBERS

Review Time: Draw lines between the English word on the left and the corresponding translation on the right. Refer back to the original puzzle if you need help.

E	E	I	G	H	T	Y	Π	N	O	I	L	L	I	M	S
A	N	N	S	O	T	A	Y	N	E	E	T	H	G	I	E
T	A	G	I	R	T	T	Y	A	S	E	C	A	Y	B	V
N	E	T	O	N	F	H	E	T	E	I	T	T	U	Ό	E
H	K	F	N	I	E	Δ	O	N	R	Δ	X	E	Ά	X	N
M	A	K	F	A	D	T	E	U	E	I	R	T	N	E	T
O	T	Ω	H	N	P	N	Y	K	S	B	H	I	E	I	Y
Δ	O	T	O	U	H	A	A	T	A	A	Ξ	T	Π	E	N
B	M	X	S	N	N	E	Σ	A	N	E	N	E	Γ	A	N
E	M	O	T	O	Φ	D	T	Δ	A	E	N	D	T	I	B
T	Y	A	Y	T	A	M	R	K	V	H	W	N	P	E	T
Ю	P	K	A	A	A	A	E	E	N	Ξ	O	T	I	T	H
E	I	E	E	K	P	Δ	S	T	D	Δ	P	K	A	A	Φ
B	O	Δ	M	E	E	W	A	P	Γ	H	H	S	N	E	N
A	T	N	H	Ξ	E	I	K	O	Σ	I	B	E	T	Y	B
B	O	H	Ψ	W	K	Π	M	T	X	I	Λ	I	A	M	T

SIXTEEN	ΕΚΑΤΟ
SEVENTEEN	ΣΑΡΑΝΤΑ
EIGHTEEN	ΤΡΙΑΝΤΑ
NINETEEN	ΔΕΚΑΕΦΤΑ
TWENTY	ΕΝΕΝΗΝΤΑ
THIRTY	ΔΕΚΑΕΝΝΙΑ
FORTY	ΔΕΚΑΕΞΙ
FIFTY	ΧΙΛΙΑ
SIXTY	ΕΒΔΟΜΗΝΤΑ
SEVENTY	ΠΕΝΗΝΤΑ
EIGHTY	ΕΙΚΟΣΙ
NINETY	ΔΕΚΑΟΧΤΩ
HUNDRED	ΟΓΔΟΝΤΑ
THOUSAND	ΕΝΑ ΕΚΑΤΟΜΜΥΡΙΟ
MILLION	ΕΞΗΝΤΑ

REVIEW: DAYS OF THE WEEK

Review Jumble: The translations in the word list below have been scrambled. Draw lines between the left and right columns to find the correct translations.

N	Y	Π	E	A	A	Y	P	I	O	E	Δ	H	O	T
A	Σ	A	B	B	A	T	O	K	Y	P	I	A	K	O
T	A	P	Δ	E	Y	T	E	P	A	X	I	I	I	Σ
I	O	A	O	T	A	B	B	A	Σ	Γ	Θ	Γ	Ω	H
O	H	Σ	M	K	K	X	H	T	P	A	T	E	T	M
N	H	K	A	I	P	Y	K	A	A	E	P	Π	Σ	E
A	O	E	Δ	Y	K	Y	H	W	D	T	M	E	O	P
L	H	Y	A	K	A	K	E	F	H	E	Д	S	M	A
H	T	H	S	D	I	D	R	U	Π	W	D	A	Ξ	H
O	U	H	N	N	N	I	R	I	E	Y	N	T	T	T
L	E	U	Θ	E	D	S	U	E	A	H	E	U	O	I
I	S	E	S	A	D	C	K	D	T	S	K	R	Ύ	P
D	D	D	Y	A	D	N	O	M	O	S	E	D	T	T
A	A	P	Y	E	H	T	O	Д	P	Ύ	E	A	Φ	X
Y	Y	Y	W	O	R	R	O	M	O	T	W	Y	E	L

MONDAY
TUESDAY
WEDNESDAY
THURSDAY
FRIDAY
SATURDAY
SUNDAY
WEEKEND
NATIONAL HOLIDAY
TODAY
TOMORROW
YESTERDAY
WEEK
DAY

ΚΥΡΙΑΚΗ
ΗΜΕΡΑ
ΔΕΥΤΕΡΑ
ΑΥΡΙΟ
ΕΘΝΙΚΗ ΑΡΓΙΑ
ΣΑΒΒΑΤΟ
ΤΕΤΑΡΤΗ
ΤΡΙΤΗ
ΠΑΡΑΣΚΕΥΗ
ΕΒΔΟΜΑΔΑ
ΠΕΜΠΤΗ
ΣΑΒΒΑΤΟΚΥΡΙΑΚΟ
ΣΗΜΕΡΑ
ΧΘΕΣ

REVIEW: MONTHS

Review Time: Draw lines between the English word on the left and the corresponding translation on the right. Refer back to the original puzzle if you need help.

Α Σ Ο Ι Ρ Β Μ Ε Κ Ε Δ Υ Υ Φ Ν Υ
Υ Α Θ Κ Ο C T O B E R A Y O R L
Γ Η Π Η Τ Τ Η C R A M H E A A U
Ο Ο S P R Ω E N U J T M U P E J
Υ Φ Μ Μ Ι Ε Β R A N B N A R Y A
Σ Η Δ Η D Λ Β Ρ Ο Ρ Α Ο G Ι Σ Β
T O M N N E I M I J E V S L E P
Ο Ώ Ι Ε F A C O E O M E A E Π T
Σ Χ Γ Ρ Ρ Ό Σ Ε Σ Τ Σ Μ U L T Σ
V T P T A O T O M H P B G Ώ E I
Φ Α Ο Ο Ι Υ Λ Υ Ι Β Ξ Ε U A M S
Ψ Α Ι Λ Ν Ε Ο Ο Κ Τ Ε R S I B C
Ι Ο Υ Ν Ι Ο Σ Ν Γ Ι Ρ R T E P C
Σ Ο Ι Α Μ Ά Σ Η Α Ι S A P C I I
Ι Φ Ε Β Ρ Ο Υ Α Ρ Ι Ο Σ Μ Ρ Ο Ν
E C A R A D N E L A C W X O Σ B

JANUARY	ΟΚΤΩΒΡΙΟΣ
FEBRUARY	ΔΕΚΕΜΒΡΙΟΣ
MARCH	ΜΑΙΟΣ
APRIL	ΗΜΕΡΟΛΟΓΙΟ
MAY	ΙΟΥΛΙΟΣ
JUNE	ΑΠΡΙΛΙΟΣ
JULY	ΝΟΕΜΒΡΙΟΣ
AUGUST	ΧΡΟΝΟΣ
SEPTEMBER	ΜΑΡΤΙΟΣ
OCTOBER	ΦΕΒΡΟΥΑΡΙΟΣ
NOVEMBER	ΜΗΝΑΣ
DECEMBER	ΣΕΠΤΕΜΒΡΙΟΣ
CALENDAR	ΙΑΝΟΥΑΡΙΟΣ
MONTH	ΑΥΓΟΥΣΤΟΣ
YEAR	ΙΟΥΝΙΟΣ

REVIEW: TIME & SEASONS

Review Jumble: The translations in the word list below have been scrambled. Draw lines between the left and right columns to find the correct translations.

<table>
<tr><td>O</td><td>R</td><td>U</td><td>O</td><td>H</td><td>G</td><td>O</td><td>D</td><td>E</td><td>C</td><td>A</td><td>D</td><td>E</td><td>H</td><td>Λ</td></tr>
<tr><td>Ό</td><td>R</td><td>E</td><td>T</td><td>N</td><td>I</td><td>W</td><td>P</td><td>Ώ</td><td>B</td><td>Ψ</td><td>S</td><td>Ί</td><td>E</td><td>Δ</td></tr>
<tr><td>Ύ</td><td>Д</td><td>N</td><td>I</td><td>X</td><td>Δ</td><td>M</td><td>N</td><td>Ω</td><td>Π</td><td>H</td><td>V</td><td>Π</td><td>E</td><td>E</td></tr>
<tr><td>D</td><td>O</td><td>R</td><td>Y</td><td>N</td><td>E</td><td>I</td><td>O</td><td>P</td><td>Π</td><td>O</td><td>T</td><td>K</td><td>D</td><td>T</td></tr>
<tr><td>M</td><td>P</td><td>E</td><td>O</td><td>O</td><td>Y</td><td>I</td><td>Ω</td><td>R</td><td>E</td><td>O</td><td>A</td><td>X</td><td>H</td><td>U</td></tr>
<tr><td>S</td><td>A</td><td>M</td><td>Я</td><td>O</td><td>T</td><td>I</td><td>M</td><td>Λ</td><td>N</td><td>E</td><td>N</td><td>G</td><td>L</td><td>N</td></tr>
<tr><td>R</td><td>S</td><td>M</td><td>C</td><td>N</td><td>E</td><td>T</td><td>P</td><td>Ω</td><td>T</td><td>I</td><td>I</td><td>I</td><td>C</td><td>I</td></tr>
<tr><td>T</td><td>N</td><td>U</td><td>E</td><td>R</td><td>P</td><td>I</td><td>P</td><td>I</td><td>N</td><td>N</td><td>N</td><td>Я</td><td>Θ</td><td>M</td></tr>
<tr><td>Γ</td><td>M</td><td>S</td><td>N</td><td>E</td><td>O</td><td>D</td><td>A</td><td>Ω</td><td>A</td><td>A</td><td>T</td><td>G</td><td>X</td><td>Φ</td></tr>
<tr><td>I</td><td>U</td><td>E</td><td>T</td><td>T</td><td>Λ</td><td>X</td><td>N</td><td>T</td><td>W</td><td>K</td><td>Σ</td><td>P</td><td>I</td><td>Ψ</td></tr>
<tr><td>O</td><td>T</td><td>C</td><td>U</td><td>F</td><td>E</td><td>Ύ</td><td>O</td><td>H</td><td>X</td><td>P</td><td>O</td><td>N</td><td>O</td><td>Σ</td></tr>
<tr><td>Y</td><td>U</td><td>O</td><td>R</td><td>A</td><td>Π</td><td>P</td><td>I</td><td>H</td><td>M</td><td>Y</td><td>E</td><td>Λ</td><td>B</td><td>N</td></tr>
<tr><td>C</td><td>A</td><td>N</td><td>Y</td><td>L</td><td>T</td><td>T</td><td>Ξ</td><td>T</td><td>T</td><td>E</td><td>N</td><td>Д</td><td>A</td><td>X</td></tr>
<tr><td>Φ</td><td>S</td><td>D</td><td>T</td><td>Ό</td><td>O</td><td>M</td><td>H</td><td>N</td><td>A</td><td>Σ</td><td>P</td><td>Д</td><td>P</td><td>K</td></tr>
<tr><td>Σ</td><td>A</td><td>N</td><td>Ω</td><td>I</td><td>A</td><td>Π</td><td>O</td><td>Γ</td><td>E</td><td>Y</td><td>M</td><td>A</td><td>Ω</td><td>T</td></tr>
</table>

<table>
<tr><td>WINTER</td><td>ΔΕΥΤΕΡΟΛΕΠΤΟ</td></tr>
<tr><td>SPRING</td><td>ΚΑΛΟΚΑΙΡΙ</td></tr>
<tr><td>SUMMER</td><td>ΑΠΟΓΕΥΜΑ</td></tr>
<tr><td>AUTUMN</td><td>ΑΝΟΙΞΗ</td></tr>
<tr><td>SECOND</td><td>ΠΡΩΙ</td></tr>
<tr><td>MINUTE</td><td>ΗΜΕΡΑ</td></tr>
<tr><td>HOUR</td><td>ΝΥΧΤΑ</td></tr>
<tr><td>DAY</td><td>ΜΗΝΑΣ</td></tr>
<tr><td>MONTH</td><td>ΧΡΟΝΟΣ</td></tr>
<tr><td>YEAR</td><td>ΛΕΠΤΟ</td></tr>
<tr><td>MORNING</td><td>ΧΕΙΜΩΝΑΣ</td></tr>
<tr><td>AFTERNOON</td><td>ΑΙΩΝΑΣ</td></tr>
<tr><td>NIGHT</td><td>ΔΕΚΑΕΤΙΑ</td></tr>
<tr><td>DECADE</td><td>ΦΘΙΝΟΠΩΡΟ</td></tr>
<tr><td>CENTURY</td><td>ΩΡΑ</td></tr>
</table>

REVIEW: COLORS

Review Time: Draw lines between the English word on the left and the corresponding translation on the right. Refer back to the original puzzle if you need help.

E	I	I	E	I	M	H	Σ	A	P	B	N	Ю	E	N
Ό	Λ	Φ	N	A	N	Ω	N	Σ	T	Y	T	M	Ώ	S
I	A	Π	Y	Δ	E	C	B	Π	T	O	T	X	N	Z
K	K	P	M	A	E	Ω	P	P	P	Д	E	Y	C	O
M	O	I	Z	A	Λ	A	Γ	O	Y	B	P	H	Γ	P
K	T	N	A	H	Σ	S	Z	A	N	E	X	R	W	K
S	P	O	I	I	I	D	I	D	U	P	R	K	U	W
R	O	K	N	P	Ξ	Д	W	L	Y	H	A	G	F	O
P	Π	O	E	K	T	Y	B	Σ	V	I	U	T	A	L
Ί	H	K	L	Γ	N	I	O	Y	O	E	O	I	B	L
Δ	Λ	K	N	E	E	E	K	Φ	P	U	R	P	L	E
Ύ	N	I	M	P	T	R	E	D	C	Y	A	N	A	Y
P	P	N	O	I	H	A	B	R	O	W	N	E	C	X
Ю	G	O	H	N	Ώ	D	L	O	G	G	G	A	K	T
A	D	W	Д	K	I	O	H	M	A	G	E	N	T	A

BLACK
BLUE
BROWN
CYAN
GOLD
GREY
GREEN
MAGENTA
ORANGE
PINK
PURPLE
RED
SILVER
WHITE
YELLOW

ΚΑΦΕ
ΚΙΤΡΙΝΟ
ΦΟΥΞΙΑ
ΜΩΒ
ΓΑΛΑΖΙΟ
ΑΣΠΡΟ
ΠΟΡΤΟΚΑΛΙ
ΑΣΗΜΙ
ΧΡΥΣΟ
ΠΡΑΣΙΝΟ
ΡΟΖ
ΓΚΡΙ
ΚΟΚΚΙΝΟ
ΜΑΥΡΟ
ΜΠΛΕ

REVIEW: SHAPES

Review Jumble: The translations in the word list below have been scrambled. Draw lines between the left and right columns to find the correct translations.

D	I	M	A	R	Y	P	H	Y	A	P	I	A	Φ	Σ
I	H	O	T	E	T	O	K	T	A	Γ	Ω	N	O	V
A	E	B	N	T	L	Y	I	N	Ό	X	I	N	P	C
M	X	A	W	Ω	K	C	T	N	O	B	Ω	F	Y	K
O	A	Λ	T	Λ	Γ	R	R	N	Ω	Γ	Ω	L	Ω	K
N	G	A	O	E	I	A	Ω	I	A	Γ	I	N	Y	Σ
D	O	Σ	Δ	A	L	Γ	T	Ξ	C	N	O	Λ	E	O
B	N	G	N	I	A	G	E	N	D	Σ	I	Θ	T	B
Ό	X	G	A	P	M	C	N	E	E	N	Д	D	P	M
Σ	L	Γ	T	T	A	A	R	A	Δ	Π	C	S	I	O
E	O	E	L	Ю	N	E	P	P	T	E	U	Q	Γ	P
E	T	B	H	A	H	E	O	Y	O	C	B	U	Ω	Ώ
I	M	Π	Y	P	V	Σ	P	Ό	Π	N	E	A	N	Я
R	A	T	S	K	N	O	G	A	T	C	O	R	O	R
U	P	I	I	P	E	T	Σ	A	C	O	N	E	Ό	Ψ

CIRCLE	ΠΥΡΑΜΙΔΑ
CONE	ΕΞΑΓΩΝΟ
CUBE	ΑΣΤΕΡΙ
CYLINDER	ΚΩΝΟΣ
DIAMOND	ΡΟΜΒΟΣ
HEXAGON	ΚΥΛΙΝΔΡΟΣ
OCTAGON	ΚΥΒΟΣ
OVAL	ΣΦΑΙΡΑ
PENTAGON	ΤΡΙΓΩΝΟ
PYRAMID	ΠΕΝΤΑΓΩΝΟ
RECTANGLE	ΟΚΤΑΓΩΝΟ
SPHERE	ΤΕΤΡΑΓΩΝΟ
SQUARE	ΟΒΑΛ
STAR	ΚΥΚΛΟΣ
TRIANGLE	ΟΡΘΟΓΩΝΙΟ

REVIEW: THE HEAD

Review Time: Draw lines between the English word on the left and the corresponding translation on the right. Refer back to the original puzzle if you need help.

F	A	C	E	Y	E	B	R	O	W	S	T	K	T	A
N	Ώ	B	H	Ω	N	S	P	I	L	O	E	T	Σ	Ω
I	S	O	Λ	Y	O	Γ	A	M	A	Φ	Z	Σ	Δ	B
H	E	A	D	E	L	T	Y	D	A	H	Ω	O	N	B
C	H	E	E	K	Φ	T	O	Λ	I	Λ	N	V	Ξ	X
D	S	O	T	T	H	A	I	B	Γ	T	Λ	Γ	E	Γ
Ί	A	O	Π	Ω	Σ	O	P	Π	I	Я	Ώ	I	K	T
T	L	E	X	Ω	X	L	H	A	T	T	Λ	A	A	K
E	E	Φ	H	Ό	T	Γ	X	I	Y	H	I	E	M	P
N	Y	U	P	E	O	E	Σ	N	A	I	Ώ	B	O	E
E	E	E	G	Y	R	T	M	M	Ώ	H	A	Ξ	T	R
Σ	S	A	N	N	Δ	O	E	T	I	Ό	Ξ	Θ	Σ	E
B	O	I	R	Ύ	O	I	F	T	K	O	X	Д	F	T
A	N	H	T	E	E	T	A	N	Ю	P	I	N	S	O
A	M	O	U	T	H	M	Ω	Ί	Ξ	E	E	Y	T	M

CHEEK	ΔΟΝΤΙΑ
CHIN	ΜΑΛΛΙΑ
EAR	ΣΤΟΜΑ
EYE	ΜΑΓΟΥΛΟ
EYEBROWS	ΜΑΤΙ
EYELASHES	ΒΛΕΦΑΡΑ
FACE	ΧΕΙΛΗ
FOREHEAD	ΓΛΩΣΣΑ
HAIR	ΦΡΥΔΙΑ
HEAD	ΜΥΤΗ
LIPS	ΚΕΦΑΛΙ
MOUTH	ΑΥΤΙ
NOSE	ΠΡΟΣΩΠΟ
TEETH	ΠΗΓΟΥΝΙ
TONGUE	ΜΕΤΩΠΟ

REVIEW: THE BODY

Review Jumble: The translations in the word list below have been scrambled. Draw lines between the left and right columns to find the correct translations.

Y	Δ	A	X	Σ	X	M	R	I	I	W	A	I	S	T
O	A	E	D	A	L	B	R	E	D	L	U	O	H	S
I	X	Σ	A	N	Ω	K	Γ	A	G	E	L	B	O	W
Δ	T	H	Y	Ύ	A	A	I	U	T	N	N	Y	U	Ώ
O	Y	M	T	O	E	P	Θ	S	I	K	I	Φ	L	Ί
Π	Λ	A	Θ	A	T	H	O	Δ	A	Π	P	F	D	Ψ
O	O	Λ	Ξ	S	Λ	A	O	P	H	H	P	T	E	W
Λ	X	A	Φ	H	Σ	Π	Π	T	Σ	F	L	I	R	M
Y	E	Π	D	M	M	O	O	E	E	O	E	I	H	Z
T	P	O	N	R	Σ	S	M	M	P	O	S	Ώ	M	Σ
X	I	Π	A	I	O	X	R	Ω	Ω	T	T	M	M	N
A	O	T	H	U	M	B	X	A	B	Ύ	E	G	I	M
Δ	Y	O	N	L	M	Y	E	E	Σ	F	T	E	H	F
K	T	H	K	P	Д	X	O	G	P	O	N	L	T	I
Γ	O	Φ	O	Σ	A	P	I	E	X	I	T	N	A	E

ARM	ΩΜΟΠΛΑΤΗ
ELBOW	ΔΑΧΤΥΛΟ ΠΟΔΙΟΥ
FINGER	ΩΜΟΣ
FOOT	ΠΟΔΙ
HAND	ΠΑΛΑΜΗ
HIP	ΜΕΣΗ
LEG	ΓΟΦΟΣ
NIPPLE	ΔΑΧΤΥΛΟ ΧΕΡΙΟΥ
SHOULDER	ΧΕΡΙ
SHOULDER BLADE	ΘΗΛΗ
THUMB	ΠΑΤΟΥΣΑ
TOE	ΑΝΤΙΧΕΙΡΑΣ
WAIST	ΑΓΚΩΝΑΣ
WRIST	ΚΑΡΠΟΣ

REVIEW: THE BODY 2

Review Time: Draw lines between the English word on the left and the corresponding translation on the right. Refer back to the original puzzle if you need help.

Γ A M Π A Y Σ A K A S T D A Д
A S Ί H Γ O N A T O C Θ A N L
N M E X Θ M P A H B A C K A I
Λ P Ω H T T H T Φ Ύ L N O V A
S A T Σ X I S P M T F Π K E N
K Σ P L X K Ю A O R I Я Λ L R
C T A Y I B M E E Σ A A Y X E
O P N N Γ A Y O Θ R I E N Y G
T A H N Σ Γ M I M M B E R D N
T Γ N X C Φ A P O A C N P O I
U A A Π A P I Σ U K N K U B F
B Λ Ψ Λ F T A O R H T H I G H
H O O A M P E Δ X Ό N O S K N
T Σ Z T Д F C T O I L Γ K Ψ Γ
H I N H O Ί M F M A W K O I K

ANKLE	ΠΛΑΤΗ
ARMPIT	ΜΑΣΧΑΛΗ
BACK	ΟΜΦΑΛΟΣ
BODY	ΔΕΡΜΑ
BREAST	ΣΤΗΘΟΣ
BUTTOCKS	ΜΗΡΟΣ
CALF	ΛΑΙΜΟΣ
FINGERNAIL	ΠΗΧΗΣ
FOREARM	ΑΣΤΡΑΓΑΛΟΣ
KNEE	ΓΟΝΑΤΟ
NAVEL	ΓΑΜΠΑ
NECK	ΟΠΙΣΘΙΑ
SKIN	ΝΥΧΙ
THIGH	ΣΩΜΑ
THROAT	ΛΑΡΥΓΓΑΣ

REVIEW: ON THE INSIDE

76

Review Jumble: The translations in the word list below have been scrambled. Draw lines between the left and right columns to find the correct translations.

L	Η	Σ	Π	Λ	Η	Ν	Α	Ρ	Τ	Η	Ρ	Ι	Ε	Σ	Α
S	A	E	R	C	N	A	P	N	Ν	Ύ	Χ	Ο	Ρ	Λ	Η
M	W	R	A	E	Π	N	E	Γ	Κ	Ε	Φ	Α	Λ	Ο	Σ
A	A	O	G	R	V	N	T	Σ	Υ	Ν	Φ	Ι	Ύ	Η	Η
L	O	I	Π	E	T	I	E	Θ	Υ	Ε	Χ	Ρ	Δ	Χ	Ο
L	P	C	M	Π	I	Y	L	Y	N	A	N	I	O	P	S
I	E	E	B	A	M	N	C	S	M	Q	E	D	E	E	Σ
N	T	Ψ	L	N	A	J	T	O	N	O	X	T	I	E	Y
T	N	D	O	Γ	I	Ό	T	E	K	I	N	R	B	K	K
E	E	I	O	K	Δ	Σ	E	H	S	E	E	E	B	B	Ω
S	O	I	D	P	P	L	Λ	E	Y	T	Λ	V	Σ	R	T
T	T	N	E	E	A	Ω	L	X	R	Φ	I	L	S	A	I
I	Π	A	C	A	K	C	A	A	P	P	E	N	D	I	X
N	E	H	Y	Σ	S	Π	A	X	S	P	L	E	E	N	B
E	Λ	O	O	U	Я	A	E	E	I	K	Λ	I	U	Я	H
H	C	A	M	O	T	S	G	N	U	L	Y	O	T	E	A

APPENDIX	ΣΤΟΜΑΧΙ
ARTERIES	ΛΕΠΤΟ ΕΝΤΕΡΟ
BLOOD	ΠΑΧΥ ΕΝΤΕΡΟ
BRAIN	ΠΑΝΓΚΡΕΑΣ
HEART	ΠΝΕΥΜΟΝΕΣ
KIDNEY	ΑΙΜΑ
LARGE INTESTINE	ΦΛΕΒΕΣ
LIVER	ΕΓΚΕΦΑΛΟΣ
LUNGS	ΣΠΛΗΝΑ
MUSCLES	ΣΚΩΛΗΚΟΕΙΔΗΣ αποφυση
PANCREAS	ΝΕΦΡΟ
SMALL INTESTINE	ΚΑΡΔΙΑ
SPLEEN	ΑΡΤΗΡΙΕΣ
STOMACH	ΜΥΕΣ
VEINS	ΣΥΚΩΤΙ

REVIEW: EARTH

Review Time: Draw lines between the English word on the left and the corresponding translation on the right. Refer back to the original puzzle if you need help.

A S O U T H A M E R I C A P N Σ B
A T O N H N S Σ A P E I A H O O H
N Ό Λ Ψ O Ω E Φ O L O C P T T K T
T A L A H R P N O P I R A S I H Ά
A Ό E H N I T P I F I Λ U P A M B
R E X C K T H H I T Π E E E A O O
C D L H O T I C A O N M Π A M K P
T U U O U C O K K M A O N H E I E
I T I O P C I I O A E T C Y P Φ I
C I S H E H Φ T I Σ A R P N I A O
A G B A A A T E N P Ω Ω I Д K P Σ
I N N I Γ D P R K A Π K O C H Γ Π
S O X P R O N T O H L E E E A Ω O
A L Ω Д B A I Σ A N Σ T B A Δ E Λ
L E N K O K E D U T I T A L N Γ O
Γ E I P H N I K O Σ Ω K E A N O Σ
A F R I C A N O T I O Σ Π O Λ O Σ

AFRICA	ΑΣΙΑ
ANTARCTICA	ΓΕΩΡΓΑΦΙΚΟ ΠΛΑΤΟΣ
ASIA	ΑΤΛΑΝΤΙΚΟΣ ΩΚΕΑΝΟΣ
ATLANTIC OCEAN	ΒΟΡΕΙΑ ΑΜΕΡΙΚΗ
CONTINENT	ΑΦΡΙΚΗ
EUROPE	ΓΕΩΓΡΑΦΙΚΟ ΜΗΚΟΣ
LATITUDE	ΝΟΤΙΟΣ ΠΟΛΟΣ
LONGITUDE	ΗΠΕΙΡΟΣ
NORTH AMERICA	ΑΝΤΑΡΚΤΙΚΗ
NORTH POLE	ΕΙΡΗΝΙΚΟΣ ΩΚΕΑΝΟΣ
PACIFIC OCEAN	ΕΥΡΩΠΗ
SOUTH AMERICA	ΝΟΤΙΑ ΑΜΕΡΙΚΗ
SOUTH POLE	ΒΟΡΕΙΟΣ ΠΟΛΟΣ

REVIEW: GEOGRAPHY 78

Review Jumble: The translations in the word list below have been scrambled. Draw lines between the left and right columns to find the correct translations.

Θ	Α	Λ	Α	Σ	Σ	Α	Ν	Ω	Τ	Ε	Γ	Α	Π	Δ
Π	Α	Ρ	Α	Λ	Ι	Α	Κ	R	Λ	Ε	D	Ι	Χ	Φ
Ο	Σ	Ο	Μ	Η	Ρ	Ε	Ρ	Ί	D	N	T	L	M	F
T	O	S	G	A	A	Ω	G	H	A	E	O	A	F	O
A	B	O	Y	N	O	Y	N	L	T	N	S	K	E	R
M	U	Ό	O	R	T	H	S	I	A	A	H	E	E	E
I	R	Σ	O	I	H	I	E	C	A	C	P	E	R	S
B	E	N	C	V	E	Φ	L	Δ	C	T	I	K	L	T
E	H	N	A	E	C	O	A	K	T	H	N	E	A	C
Π	T	Ω	E	R	V	Σ	H	I	F	Ώ	Λ	U	R	Φ
T	A	H	Λ	H	O	T	K	C	Σ	T	S	A	O	C
Π	Γ	Ρ	Ι	Σ	Ю	Α	Ι	Ά	Α	Τ	Τ	Θ	C	M
E	O	Ύ	M	Ψ	M	Σ	T	E	H	E	E	W	D	M
H	W	Λ	N	R	H	T	S	A	R	O	B	I	U	C
E	Q	Σ	H	N	E	Γ	O	I	Λ	Λ	A	P	O	K

BEACH	ΚΟΡΑΛΛΙΟΓΕΝΗΣ υφαλοσ
CITY	ΕΡΗΜΟΣ
COAST	ΛΙΜΝΗ
CORAL REEF	ΝΗΣΙ
CRATER	ΠΑΓΕΤΩΝΑΣ
DESERT	ΘΑΛΑΣΣΑ
FOREST	ΚΡΑΤΗΡΑΣ
GLACIER	ΩΚΕΑΝΟΣ
ISLAND	ΗΦΑΙΣΤΕΙΟ
LAKE	ΠΟΛΗ
MOUNTAIN	ΑΚΤΗ
OCEAN	ΔΑΣΟΣ
RIVER	ΠΟΤΑΜΙ
SEA	ΠΑΡΑΛΙΑ
VOLCANO	ΒΟΥΝΟ

REVIEW: WEATHER

Review Time: Draw lines between the English word on the left and the corresponding translation on the right. Refer back to the original puzzle if you need help.

H	T	Σ	E	Z	Ύ	Λ	Ο	Π	D	Σ	Δ	L	Ά	K	A
Σ	H	Σ	Y	N	N	E	Φ	I	A	Σ	M	E	N	O	Σ
E	O	D	O	A	B	P	O	N	T	H	P	E	X	Ξ	T
I	Z	E	Σ	T	H	Ψ	Ω	K	T	E	X	B	C	O	P
Π	W	T	O	N	Σ	Φ	P	Ψ	M	E	Θ	D	A	T	A
H	W	O	N	S	Y	Y	O	M	I	X	Λ	H	X	O	Π
K	C	A	B	T	O	E	O	Ю	E	Y	T	R	I	I	H
I	I	G	R	N	D	A	Ί	Λ	R	A	E	A	O	N	H
P	R	N	O	M	I	I	R	Y	O	D	N	F	N	A	S
T	T	I	Ώ	F	W	A	M	D	N	I	D	E	I	P	Λ
E	E	N	A	C	I	R	R	U	H	Θ	Λ	Σ	M	Y	Q
M	M	T	Λ	N	N	D	H	O	H	A	A	H	M	O	O
O	O	H	E	K	D	T	N	L	B	P	O	X	H	N	E
P	R	G	D	N	Y	L	T	C	Γ	O	I	I	B	E	M
A	A	I	Δ	Γ	A	A	O	Y	Д	Y	N	N	U	S	P
B	B	L	E	T	Ω	L	H	C	G	O	O	E	T	P	W

BAROMETRIC pressure	ME ANEMO
CLOUDY	XIONI
COLD	ΤΥΦΩΝΑΣ
FOG	ΗΛΙΟΛΟΥΣΤΟΣ
HOT	ΒΡΟΝΤΗ
HUMID	ΑΣΤΡΑΠΗ
HURRICANE	ΟΥΡΑΝΙΟ ΤΟΞΟ
LIGHTNING	ΥΓΡΑΣΙΑ
RAIN	ΚΡΥΟ
RAINBOW	ΖΕΣΤΗ
SNOW	ΟΜΙΧΛΗ
SUNNY	ΣΥΝΝΕΦΙΑΣΜΕΝΟΣ
THUNDER	ΠΟΛΎ ΖΕΣΤΗ
WARM	ΒΑΡΟΜΕΤΡΙΚΗ ΠΙΕΣΗ
WINDY	ΒΡΟΧΗ

REVIEW: AFRICAN ANIMALS 80

Review Jumble: The translations in the word list below have been scrambled. Draw lines between the left and right columns to find the correct translations.

Θ	Z	M	L	E	O	P	A	R	D	T	W	Ξ	Q	Σ	Y	Λ
T	Σ	E	K	S	Π	I	T	O	B	F	P	T	Σ	A	H	B
K	Σ	A	B	H	U	N	Π	Ά	E	R	Δ	O	I	Λ	A	X
A	K	T	Y	P	A	M	E	Π	H	Ό	N	N	A	Λ	P	I
K	D	E	P	H	A	Λ	A	X	O	I	A	Δ	T	I	I	M
H	N	E	P	O	L	R	E	T	Y	Π	P	M	Σ	P	N	Π
A	A	E	P	I	Y	H	H	O	O	A	O	T	I	O	O	A
T	L	Z	O	O	A	Θ	Π	I	Π	P	Я	T	T	Γ	K	N
E	L	N	E	T	L	M	O	O	N	A	O	Σ	A	Ψ	E	T
E	I	A	A	B	A	E	Λ	K	Λ	O	P	P	X	M	P	Z
H	R	P	H	Π	R	H	T	S	A	I	C	Δ	P	O	O	H
C	O	M	M	M	M	A	Σ	N	L	M	T	E	A	I	Σ	Σ
I	G	I	M	A	N	O	O	B	A	B	H	N	R	Λ	H	Θ
R	O	H	K	H	I	P	A	T	N	O	I	Λ	A	O	H	Γ
T	I	C	H	K	Φ	A	K	O	X	O	I	P	O	Σ	S	T
S	I	O	P	S	G	E	Λ	E	Φ	A	N	T	A	Σ	N	Я
O	I	K	G	I	R	A	F	F	E	G	O	H	T	R	A	W

ANTELOPE	ΑΝΤΙΛΟΠΗ
BABOON	ΧΙΜΠΑΝΤΖΗΣ
CHEETAH	ΣΤΡΟΥΘΟΚΑΜΗΛΟΣ
CHIMPANZEE	ΤΣΙΤΑΧ
ELEPHANT	ΕΛΕΦΑΝΤΑΣ
GIRAFFE	ΛΕΟΠΑΡΔΑΛΗ
GORILLA	ΜΠΑΜΠΟΥΙΝΟΣ
HIPPOPOTAMUS	ΚΑΜΗΛΟΠΑΡΔΑΛΗ
HYENA	ΖΕΒΡΑ
LEOPARD	ΙΠΠΟΠΟΤΑΜΟΣ
LION	ΡΙΝΟΚΕΡΟΣ
OSTRICH	ΛΙΟΝΤΑΡΙ
RHINOCEROS	ΓΟΡΙΛΛΑΣ
WARTHOG	ΥΑΙΝΑ
ZEBRA	ΦΑΚΟΧΟΙΡΟΣ

REVIEW: ANIMAL KINGDOM 1

Review Time: Draw lines between the English word on the left and the corresponding translation on the right. Refer back to the original puzzle if you need help.

A E N O E Δ R I Я Ώ E S U O M
Ί I D Y T K T R E G I T A B U
A Λ H M A K E E D G Σ Z E X L
T Δ Π I N Γ K O Y I N O Σ T E
Φ T Y Y O Π E Λ A N M P Γ Z H
K M C O N P N Δ Y O Λ Y T A K
Π A Ξ Я K I I K Y P Y O H Γ Λ
E O N S U P M Λ O Σ K K R K A
Ξ T N G E J A L C H O Γ P O M
H H N T A P A H M P Σ N X Y M
B E X G I R K O K Γ K A K A I
P Y U T B K O W G I Y K T P P
N A A E T S I O T T Λ Ώ Θ A A
R C A M E L D L X T O O I L Γ
D R A B B I T F O X Σ T Π A X

BAT	ΑΛΕΠΟΥ
CAMEL	ΤΙΓΡΗΣ
CAT	ΛΥΚΟΣ
DOG	ΜΟΥΛΑΡΙ
FOX	ΣΚΥΛΟΣ
JAGUAR	ΑΛΚΗ
KANGAROO	ΠΟΝΤΙΚΙ
MOOSE	ΓΑΤΑ
MOUSE	ΠΟΛΙΚΗ ΑΡΚΟΥΔΑ
MULE	ΚΑΜΗΛΑ
PENGUIN	ΤΖΑΓΚΟΥΑΡ
POLAR BEAR	ΠΙΝΓΚΟΥΙΝΟΣ
RABBIT	ΛΑΓΟΣ
TIGER	ΚΑΝΓΚΟΥΡΟ
WOLF	ΝΥΧΤΕΡΙΔΑ

REVIEW: ANIMAL KINGDOM 2 (82)

Review Jumble: The translations in the word list below have been scrambled. Draw lines between the left and right columns to find the correct translations.

P	Σ	O	I	A	P	Y	O	P	A	T	A	M	A	L	L
Σ	O	C	N	Σ	I	A	I	Π	R	A	C	C	O	O	N
O	P	R	S	Σ	O	Γ	K	K	Я	R	M	Φ	I	Δ	I
P	O	O	C	E	O	Π	A	O	A	A	X	Y	C	Ψ	D
Y	S	C	B	U	A	K	Ω	B	Y	P	I	G	A	K	Σ
O	S	O	A	M	P	R	Γ	P	Y	N	Y	K	P	N	A
I	U	D	T	M	B	I	H	A	Θ	O	A	O	A	M	P
K	M	I	P	Ω	K	A	N	B	T	N	K	M	I	Σ	O
Σ	Ί	L	A	T	P	M	L	E	Θ	O	Ά	Y	A	K	T
Φ	Y	E	X	K	Y	A	K	O	Δ	K	K	I	O	Λ	Σ
Π	Ω	R	O	O	C	A	X	E	N	O	G	A	Λ	K	A
E	A	Y	Σ	K	N	O	I	U	T	X	L	O	P	A	K
I	Δ	O	B	S	I	Λ	K	B	E	A	V	E	R	Y	Π
A	Π	E	P	P	O	S	Q	U	I	R	R	E	L	F	O
O	A	I	O	Σ	N	A	T	U	G	N	A	R	O	W	L
R	B	Σ	T	T	T	C	C	H	I	P	M	U	N	K	Ύ

BEAVER	ΚΑΣΤΟΡΑΣ
BLACK BEAR	ΛΑΜΑ
CHIPMUNK	ΜΑΥΡΗ ΑΡΚΟΥΔΑ
CROCODILE	ΟΥΡΑΚΟΤΑΓΚΟΣ
FROG	ΡΑΚΟΥΝ
LLAMA	ΚΡΟΚΟΔΕΙΛΟΣ
OPOSSUM	ΒΑΤΡΑΧΟΣ
ORANGUTAN	ΑΡΟΥΡΑΙΟΣ
OWL	ΣΚΙΟΥΡΟΣ
PORCUPINE	ΚΟΥΚΟΥΒΑΓΙΑ
RACCOON	ΑΚΑΝΘΟΧΟΙΡΟΣ
RAT	ΟΠΟΣΟΥΜ
SKUNK	ΠΑΛΙΆΝΘΡΩΠΟΣ
SNAKE	ΦΙΔΙ
SQUIRREL	ΣΚΙΟΥΡΑΚΙ

REVIEW: SEA LIFE

Review Time: Draw lines between the English word on the left and the corresponding translation on the right. Refer back to the original puzzle if you need help.

N	Θ	Σ	O	Π	Π	I	Σ	O	I	Σ	Σ	A	Λ	A	Θ
Ψ	A	P	I	O	N	T	E	H	F	B	C	Σ	A	N	S
M	Λ	Λ	A	Δ	A	N	B	I	C	O	E	T	P	J	Q
Ώ	Ά	M	Ύ	Φ	H	P	S	N	B	I	P	A	T	E	U
L	Σ	M	X	O	A	H	T	T	O	C	X	K	P	L	I
T	Σ	C	Z	T	Π	Λ	E	X	A	I	Ά	O	A	L	D
Σ	I	P	A	M	A	Λ	A	K	Y	R	L	Σ	N	Y	D
L	O	A	C	R	O	Π	Π	I	E	O	F	A	N	F	U
I	Λ	A	A	R	A	O	O	T	N	L	Σ	I	E	I	E
P	I	K	I	N	A	I	S	Δ	A	A	H	T	S	S	E
T	O	A	K	R	Ω	B	E	E	I	P	E	L	A	H	W
O	N	B	Ω	R	O	Λ	S	P	L	T	E	O	M	O	Ώ
Δ	T	O	Φ	L	Φ	Y	E	O	C	T	O	P	U	S	X
A	Ά	Y	M	I	Θ	T	D	X	K	K	R	A	H	S	T
Q	P	P	N	K	Σ	E	X	W	A	L	R	U	S	M	Φ
A	I	I	Σ	A	I	P	A	X	P	A	K	Λ	T	O	N

TURTLE
CRAB
DOLPHIN
FISH
JELLYFISH
LOBSTER
OCTOPUS
ORCA
SEA LION
SEAL
SHARK
SQUID
STARFISH
WALRUS
WHALE

ΑΣΤΕΡΙΑΣ
ΧΤΑΠΟΔΙ
ΦΑΛΑΙΝΑ
ΔΕΛΦΙΝΙ
ΘΑΛΑΣΣΙΟΣ ΙΠΠΟΣ
ΚΑΒΟΥΡΙ
ΟΡΚΑ
ΤΣΟΥΧΤΡΑ
ΚΑΛΑΜΑΡΙ
ΨΑΡΙ
ΧΕΛΩΝΑ
ΑΣΤΑΚΟΣ
ΚΑΡΧΑΡΙΑΣ
ΦΩΚΙΑ
ΘΑΛΆΣΣΙΟ ΛΙΟΝΤΆΡΙ

REVIEW: FAMILY 1

Review Jumble: The translations in the word list below have been scrambled. Draw lines between the left and right columns to find the correct translations.

P	Θ	H	M	K	W	N	E	B	M	T	P	P	P	Δ
S	E	E	T	Ψ	O	E	K	S	O	I	H	D	H	H
A	I	W	I	K	N	P	H	M	T	Φ	Ξ	T	I	C
Π	A	Π	Π	O	Y	Σ	H	P	H	N	Ώ	T	A	L
A	I	Δ	Σ	T	Σ	T	A	K	E	Γ	E	N	G	D
I	E	Ώ	E	I	E	Π	I	P	R	N	H	R	R	X
Δ	N	H	Φ	P	E	Δ	A	Ό	E	Ψ	B	E	A	T
I	E	Ψ	A	K	Φ	N	P	I	I	T	H	V	N	P
A	Γ	B	E	Ψ	E	O	O	O	Γ	T	A	U	D	C
N	O	R	L	C	T	Y	Σ	Γ	A	A	A	Π	M	Θ
H	K	O	C	X	E	L	Z	F	Σ	O	I	Γ	O	O
Ψ	I	T	N	O	S	I	S	T	E	R	H	Γ	T	Θ
I	O	H	U	O	Y	M	N	E	R	D	L	I	H	C
A	X	E	N	A	E	A	D	A	U	G	H	T	E	R
E	G	R	A	N	D	F	A	T	H	E	R	B	R	E

AUNT	ΑΔΕΡΦΗ
BROTHER	ΠΑΠΠΟΥΣ
CHILDREN	ΠΑΤΕΡΑΣ
DAUGHTER	ΓΙΑΓΙΑ
FAMILY	ΓΟΝΕΙΣ
FATHER	ΘΕΙΟΣ
GRANDFATHER	ΜΗΤΕΡΑ
GRANDMOTHER	ΓΙΟΣ
MOTHER	ΘΕΙΑ
NEPHEW	ΠΑΙΔΙΑ
NIECE	ΚΟΡΗ
PARENTS	ΑΔΕΡΦΟΣ
SISTER	ΟΙΚΟΓΕΝΕΙΑ
SON	ΑΝΗΨΙΟΣ
UNCLE	ΑΝΗΨΙΑ

REVIEW: FAMILY 2

Review Time: Draw lines between the English word on the left and the corresponding translation on the right. Refer back to the original puzzle if you need help.

A M K P A Γ O P I O Σ Ί Π S D P
T P K O Y N I A Δ A I E X Γ Д C
Π Θ T Σ Y Z Y Γ O Σ Θ W I F E S
E R Π C Π N A O T E A N W R Ύ I
Θ A E M E M I I P L C A G B Σ S
E F I T Π C P A N Ω L C R A Y T
P S A P H O Я I Δ N M O A B Z E
O B O T K G R A I O T U N Y Y R
Σ Σ T X H E U R H H Σ S D O Γ I
O Δ I Y H E E A E Д H I S B O N
N Δ Ώ T O T R R D U O N O N Σ L
O Y O H H P I I S D X P N Z R A
Γ M Φ G Я N S B N B N Σ Ю I Π W
Γ Д U H L Γ A O A L Π A G O O M
E A W A L N I N O S A M R T B M
D E W T D H N O Γ Γ E W O G E Д

BROTHER-IN-LAW	ΠΕΘΕΡΑ
BABY	ΠΕΘΕΡΟΣ
BOY	ΚΟΥΝΙΑΔΑ
COUSIN	ΕΓΓΟΝΟΣ
DAUGHTER-IN-LAW	ΑΓΟΡΙ
FATHER-IN-LAW	ΣΥΖΥΓΟΣ
GIRL	ΚΟΥΝΙΑΔΟΣ
GRANDDAUGHTER	ДВОЮРОДНАЯ СЕСТРА
GRANDSON	ΚΟΡΙΤΣΙ
HUSBAND	ΝΥΦΗ
MOTHER-IN-LAW	ΜΩΡΟ
SISTER-IN-LAW	ΕΓΓΟΝΗ
SON-IN-LAW	ΓΑΜΠΡΟΣ
WIFE	ΣΥΖΥΓΟΣ

REVIEW: VERBS 1

86

Review Jumble: The translations in the word list below have been scrambled. Draw lines between the left and right columns to find the correct translations.

N	W	O	L	L	O	F	O	T	O	C	A	R	R	Y
K	Σ	K	E	Φ	T	O	M	A	I	Ω	Z	K	W	E
E	T	R	E	T	O	S	I	N	G	T	S	L	K	T
P	E	E	L	S	O	T	R	T	O	A	Ά	E	O	Ύ
C	G	B	A	H	T	H	O	B	O	Ξ	V	P	T	M
S	N	Z	Ω	G	M	S	E	T	O	W	A	I	T	Π
Π	A	Ω	Θ	Λ	E	I	T	A	H	Y	P	M	E	Λ
E	H	Π	Y	E	A	P	A	Ω	R	I	K	Ω	Ύ	H
P	C	E	O	O	A	B	Z	M	Ω	X	N	Ύ	T	P
I	O	Λ	Λ	Γ	K	A	Y	Z	I	T	Ω	K	T	Ω
M	T	B	O	Q	Λ	A	A	O	X	E	E	O	Y	N
E	N	Y	K	Λ	I	B	L	P	K	K	E	O	Ω	Ω
N	Δ	I	A	M	A	M	I	O	K	A	E	C	I	Ω
Ω	Y	E	P	I	E	Γ	A	M	T	Γ	L	O	I	P
O	Z	K	Δ	L	L	Γ	D	A	E	R	O	T	W	T

TO ASK	ΡΩΤΩ
TO BE	ΣΚΕΦΤΟΜΑΙ
TO CARRY	ΚΟΥΒΑΛΩ
TO CHANGE	ΑΚΟΥΩ
TO COOK	ΠΕΡΙΜΕΝΩ
TO EAT	ΒΛΕΠΩ
TO FOLLOW	ΤΡΑΓΟΥΔΩ
TO HEAR	ΔΙΑΒΑΖΩ
TO PAY	ΑΚΟΛΟΥΘΩ
TO READ	ΑΛΛΑΖΩ
TO SEE	ΜΑΓΕΙΡΕΥΩ
TO SING	ΤΡΩΩ
TO SLEEP	ΕΙΜΑΙ
TO THINK	ΠΛΗΡΩΝΩ
TO WAIT	ΚΟΙΜΑΜΑΙ

REVIEW: VERBS 2

Review Time: Draw lines between the English word on the left and the corresponding translation on the right. Refer back to the original puzzle if you need help.

<table>
<tr><td>N</td><td>S</td><td>Γ</td><td>D</td><td>N</td><td>A</td><td>T</td><td>S</td><td>R</td><td>E</td><td>D</td><td>N</td><td>U</td><td>O</td><td>T</td></tr>
<tr><td>I</td><td>A</td><td>M</td><td>T</td><td>E</td><td>H</td><td>N</td><td>O</td><td>Я</td><td>D</td><td>N</td><td>I</td><td>F</td><td>O</td><td>T</td></tr>
<tr><td>T</td><td>O</td><td>W</td><td>O</td><td>R</td><td>K</td><td>P</td><td>Ό</td><td>D</td><td>K</td><td>P</td><td>K</td><td>T</td><td>K</td><td>B</td></tr>
<tr><td>T</td><td>O</td><td>D</td><td>R</td><td>I</td><td>N</td><td>K</td><td>Ξ</td><td>A</td><td>O</td><td>A</td><td>R</td><td>E</td><td>O</td><td>O</td></tr>
<tr><td>O</td><td>O</td><td>C</td><td>Я</td><td>T</td><td>M</td><td>T</td><td>E</td><td>E</td><td>N</td><td>A</td><td>Π</td><td>S</td><td>Ω</td><td>H</td></tr>
<tr><td>L</td><td>T</td><td>C</td><td>O</td><td>J</td><td>N</td><td>P</td><td>P</td><td>Ω</td><td>V</td><td>O</td><td>A</td><td>N</td><td>Ψ</td><td>Θ</td></tr>
<tr><td>O</td><td>C</td><td>O</td><td>L</td><td>M</td><td>S</td><td>L</td><td>H</td><td>E</td><td>Y</td><td>M</td><td>I</td><td>Λ</td><td>A</td><td>Ω</td></tr>
<tr><td>O</td><td>T</td><td>E</td><td>K</td><td>O</td><td>E</td><td>I</td><td>L</td><td>Λ</td><td>V</td><td>E</td><td>E</td><td>Σ</td><td>X</td><td>T</td></tr>
<tr><td>K</td><td>O</td><td>E</td><td>T</td><td>H</td><td>S</td><td>E</td><td>Ω</td><td>Z</td><td>Λ</td><td>A</td><td>Λ</td><td>X</td><td>N</td><td>A</td></tr>
<tr><td>F</td><td>Ω</td><td>A</td><td>O</td><td>Ό</td><td>I</td><td>E</td><td>P</td><td>K</td><td>Π</td><td>E</td><td>H</td><td>Y</td><td>Ω</td><td>Ξ</td></tr>
<tr><td>O</td><td>N</td><td>T</td><td>H</td><td>Ά</td><td>V</td><td>A</td><td>I</td><td>X</td><td>Σ</td><td>A</td><td>U</td><td>O</td><td>O</td><td>I</td></tr>
<tr><td>R</td><td>I</td><td>H</td><td>T</td><td>O</td><td>S</td><td>E</td><td>L</td><td>L</td><td>O</td><td>I</td><td>I</td><td>N</td><td>T</td><td>Δ</td></tr>
<tr><td>Ξ</td><td>Π</td><td>E</td><td>L</td><td>R</td><td>T</td><td>K</td><td>X</td><td>Я</td><td>O</td><td>M</td><td>P</td><td>P</td><td>E</td><td>E</td></tr>
<tr><td>Ώ</td><td>T</td><td>O</td><td>T</td><td>A</td><td>K</td><td>E</td><td>Ω</td><td>Π</td><td>A</td><td>Γ</td><td>A</td><td>B</td><td>N</td><td>Y</td></tr>
<tr><td>H</td><td>T</td><td>Ξ</td><td>M</td><td>K</td><td>A</td><td>T</td><td>A</td><td>Λ</td><td>A</td><td>B</td><td>A</td><td>I</td><td>N</td><td>Ω</td></tr>
</table>

TO CLOSE	ΜΙΛΑΩ
TO COME	ΚΑΤΑΛΑΒΑΙΝΩ
TO DO	ΕΧΩ
TO DRINK	ΤΑΞΙΔΕΥΩ
TO FIND	ΠΑΙΡΝΩ
TO HAVE	ΠΟΥΛΩ
TO HELP	ΚΑΝΩ
TO LOOK FOR	ΔΟΥΛΕΥΩ
TO LOVE	ΨΑΧΝΩ
TO SELL	ΕΡΧΟΜΑΙ
TO SPEAK	ΠΙΝΩ
TO TAKE	ΒΡΙΣΚΩ
TO TRAVEL	ΚΛΕΙΝΩ
TO UNDERSTAND	ΑΓΑΠΩ
TO WORK	ΒΟΗΘΩ

REVIEW: VERBS 3

Review Jumble: The translations in the word list below have been scrambled. Draw lines between the left and right columns to find the correct translations.

E V I G O T N A W O T O R U N
O T T K Θ R O O T O W A L K M
Y Ю Ю O A M N W L O Φ E Y Γ Ω
U Y Ά E P K F H R Д L T Π O Z
B A L Δ O L Ψ P H I E E T S I
O O Γ T O D A N C E T E A M A
T A N O I Γ Ω Y O O L E A V Π
O Γ Ω Ю P P Ω Д G B D Θ T E E
O T P H I A I O A D A D P I T
P Ω I C T Φ Z E H I Ώ Π Y R K
E X Z Σ T Ω B Ω N I A Γ H Π Ω
N E Ω A A O P Ω R T Θ T O Ω Ό
S P N Z T X O O Ω Y E P O X N
X T I D N H Ю W Π R Λ Д O T Ω
B I Δ A M O E C E M Ω H Θ A K

TO BE ABLE TO	ΠΑΙΖΩ
TO BUY	ΠΗΓΑΙΝΩ
TO DANCE	ΔΙΝΩ
TO GIVE	ΤΡΕΧΩ
TO GO	ΑΓΟΡΑΖΩ
TO KNOW	ΓΝΩΡΙΖΩ
TO LEARN	ΦΕΥΓΩ
TO LEAVE	ΠΕΡΠΑΤΩ
TO OPEN	ΧΡΩΣΤΑΩ
TO OWE	ΧΟΡΕΥΩ
TO PLAY	ΘΕΛΩ
TO RUN	ΓΡΑΦΩ
TO WALK	ΜΠΟΡΩ
TO WANT	ΑΝΟΙΓΩ
TO WRITE	ΜΑΘΑΙΝΩ

REVIEW: FOOD 1

Review Time: Draw lines between the English word on the left and the corresponding translation on the right. Refer back to the original puzzle if you need help.

O	C	A	S	E	N	Я	A	W	L	B	M	X	Σ	A
S	H	Ό	N	Ψ	Ω	M	I	I	F	T	S	Ψ	B	U
R	E	T	T	U	B	Φ	Д	R	E	Ύ	R	D	R	X
I	E	L	Ξ	Ά	P	R	U	O	L	F	A	A	D	N
C	S	O	B	O	P	I	E	P	P	L	G	K	Y	Ξ
E	E	A	Y	A	T	R	B	A	A	K	U	I	A	Y
C	R	T	O	A	T	O	E	S	D	Y	S	N	I	E
H	A	F	I	C	Y	E	Λ	T	G	T	W	A	N	S
O	T	W	Z	T	Σ	Σ	G	A	A	G	Ю	X	H	Σ
C	A	A	Y	Γ	A	Θ	I	E	H	W	E	A	G	U
O	Λ	P	P	E	Λ	Λ	M	P	V	T	Λ	Λ	Ώ	X
L	O	I	P	X	A	N	A	I	Y	E	S	T	Ύ	O
A	K	K	H	Γ	T	X	E	Γ	Y	T	I	T	Ύ	O
T	O	I	T	Φ	A	K	I	P	A	M	Y	Z	B	Λ
E	Σ	A	Ά	Z	A	I	I	Ξ	O	B	M	I	L	K

BREAD
BUTTER
CHEESE
CHOCOLATE
EGGS
FLOUR
FRUIT
MEAT
MILK
PASTA
RICE
SALAD
SUGAR
VEGETABLES
WATER

ΦΡΟΥΤΑ
ΑΛΕΥΡΙ
ΣΟΚΟΛΑΤΑ
ΛΑΧΑΝΙΚΑ
ΓΑΛΑ
ΒΟΥΤΥΡΟ
ΝΕΡΟ
ΡΥΖΙ
ΣΑΛΑΤΑ
ΑΥΓΑ
ΚΡΕΑΣ
ΤΥΡΙ
ΖΑΧΑΡΗ
ΖΥΜΑΡΙΚΑ
ΨΩΜΙ

REVIEW: FOOD 2

90

Review Jumble: The translations in the word list below have been scrambled. Draw lines between the left and right columns to find the correct translations.

Μ	Ζ	Χ	Β	Ψ	Γ	D	F	E	C	A	J	A	A	Y
Ο	Ι	Я	Χ	Μ	Η	Ζ	Κ	Ψ	Κ	Τ	Τ	C	Τ	Ν
Σ	Χ	Ν	Α	Α	Α	Ά	Χ	Ο	Ι	Ρ	Ι	Ν	Ο	Η
Χ	Ν	Χ	Ρ	Π	Λ	L	I	Β	Υ	W	A	D	Κ	Ύ
Α	Ι	Π	Α	Α	C	Α	Ε	Ο	Σ	Κ	Ο	Σ	Σ	U
Ρ	Ю	Ι	S	Γ	Ε	Ε	Τ	Ο	W	R	Ε	Α	Ι	Ρ
Ι	Γ	Π	Η	Ω	F	Β	Υ	Ι	Ι	Ο	Μ	Δ	Π	Ε
Σ	Λ	Ε	Λ	Τ	Я	Π	Υ	F	Ν	Ρ	Α	Μ	Μ	Ν
Ι	Τ	Ρ	Υ	Ο	Α	Ι	Γ	Ε	Ε	Λ	Ε	Ρ	Π	Α
Ο	Ι	Ι	Λ	Ε	Μ	Ω	Κ	Ρ	Ν	Υ	U	Υ	Υ	Κ
K	R	R	E	E	B	C	P	R	O	O	E	N	P	P
P	C	O	O	K	I	E	S	G	S	I	H	Z	A	R
Ε	Α	Ω	Μ	Η	R	Α	U	Β	Ρ	L	Τ	Ώ	L	Η
Α	Κ	Ι	C	E	C	R	E	A	M	F	Γ	Ε	Ζ	Ν
Σ	Ε	S	A	L	T	Ο	Λ	Υ	Ο	Π	Ο	Τ	Ο	Κ

BEEF	ΧΟΙΡΙΝΟ
BEER	ΜΠΙΣΚΟΤΑ
CAKE	ΤΟΥΡΤΑ
CHICKEN	ΜΟΣΧΑΡΙΣΙΟ ΚΡΕΑΣ
COOKIES	ΚΡΑΣΙ
HONEY	ΜΕΛΙ
ICE CREAM	ΛΑΔΙ
LAMB	ΜΠΥΡΑ
OIL	ΠΑΓΩΤΟ
PEPPER	ΑΡΝΙ
PORK	ΠΙΠΕΡΙ
SALT	ΣΟΥΠΑ
SOUP	ΑΛΑΤΙ
WINE	ΚΟΤΟΠΟΥΛΟ
YOGURT	ΓΙΑΟΥΡΤΙ

REVIEW: FRUIT 1

Review Time: Draw lines between the English word on the left and the corresponding translation on the right. Refer back to the original puzzle if you need help.

B B Ό O S E I R R E B W A R T S
B L U E B E R R I E S H H C P Ώ
C M E L O N I Λ A K O T P O Π T
E G G P L A N T Π O Y M O N E Γ
E Σ I P E A C H G O Ξ Φ Δ H Π A
P G Z A Y I Δ O P G P O A K O N
O A Y E T N W Φ R A W E K Σ N A
M X O N A D Π A O E U Σ I A I Z
E Λ Π I T I P Y T K S Q N M O T
G A P P E E Λ O M E O O O A O I
R Δ A P F E C Y P Σ R K O Δ R Λ
A I K R Σ I P A Φ A A M I A Д E
N Γ U Z R T R M N A C N E P A M
A I N P I G U G U Я T P A L E T
T E A Λ X L E M O N O Σ E N O B
E O O O P T I N O M E Λ C P A N

APRICOT
BLUEBERRIES
EGGPLANT
GRAPEFRUIT
GRAPES
LEMON
MELON
ORANGE
PEACH
PEAR
PINEAPPLE
PLUM
POMEGRANATE
STRAWBERRIES
WATERMELON

ΠΟΡΤΟΚΑΛΙ
ΡΟΔΑΚΙΝΟ
ΣΤΑΦΥΛΙΑ
ΜΕΛΙΤΖΑΝΑ
ΑΧΛΑΔΙ
ΔΑΜΑΣΚΗΝΟ
ΦΡΑΟΥΛΕΣ
ΛΕΜΟΝΙ
ΓΚΡΕΙΠΦΡΟΥΤ
ΚΑΡΠΟΥΖΙ
ΡΟΔΙ
ΠΕΠΟΝΙ
ΜΥΡΤΙΛΟ
ΑΝΑΝΑΣ
ΒΕΡΙΚΟΚΟ

REVIEW: FRUIT 2

Review Jumble: The translations in the word list below have been scrambled. Draw lines between the left and right columns to find the correct translations.

Ί O T A M O T Φ Ύ I N I H C C U Z
A P Y O M O T A B A Θ Y K O Λ O K
A A L I R E P P E P D E R T A E A
I K A Θ Y K O Λ O K U A W I L I N
N Λ G I F K Δ H O U S M P P P H T
S Я E A P S G Λ T P T E P E S R A
Δ E M S Γ E O R B S Π A Π K E A Λ
A G I F C K Π E E I Q I Y P I A O
X T L R Y A R I Π E Π U P Y R N Y
Ώ Φ A Θ R R N H Π H N E A E R A Π
A A A M I E N T N H P P K S E N E
C N P E O I B I A W N E E Ύ H A I
M A S Y Σ T K K O L P I O P C B A
O N Y A O K N L C A O H P I P P B
Δ A P Λ O E L E Σ A U U E T N E H
B Π H K F E M I T B L H P S I Z R
Ύ M I T Y E A Σ Y K O B K E A K R

APPLE	ΛΑΙΜ
BANANA	ΜΠΑΝΑΝΑ
BLACKBERRIES	ΜΗΛΟ
CANTALOUPE	ΚΟΚΚΙΝΗ ΠΙΠΕΡΙΑ
CHERRIES	ΚΑΝΤΑΛΟΥΠΕ
FIG	ΚΙΤΡΙΝΗ ΠΙΠΕΡΙΑ
GREEN PEPPER	ΣΜΕΟΥΡΑ
LIME	ΚΟΛΟΚΥΘΑ
PUMPKIN	ΚΕΡΑΣΙΑ
RASPBERRIES	ΝΤΟΜΑΤΑ
RED PEPPER	ΠΡΑΣΙΝΗ ΠΙΠΕΡΙΑ
SQUASH	ΒΑΤΟΜΟΥΡΑ
TOMATO	ΚΟΛΟΚΥΘΑ
YELLOW PEPPER	ΣΥΚΟ
ZUCCHINI	ΚΟΛΟΚΥΘΑΚΙ

REVIEW: VEGETABLES 1

Review Time: Draw lines between the English word on the left and the corresponding translation on the right. Refer back to the original puzzle if you need help.

```
P C A B B A G E L A K Σ P T M G
C I L O C C O R B E Π O O Φ Φ A
A R T I C H O K E A C R T A B R
U S P I N A C H P E R U A A Π L
L I P H M N T A Σ A N Π T Ψ B I
I E Z A N Π Γ I C K O P O T E C
F M P E R Γ P Σ Δ O O D E H E E
L A Π Π I A Π O O Y T P S A T L
O P A A O A G X K N M O Δ X S E
W O B T N W Z U Я O A M P O T R
E Y K A I T Ξ P S Y Λ X E A Θ Y
R Λ K T Λ R Z T Z Π R O A P K S
N I E E E A P A N I K Γ A Λ K G
N C E Σ Σ R T X P Δ O N I O N Φ
Π P A Σ I N A M Π I Z E Λ I A E
D H M R L A A Δ I N A X A Λ G Φ
```

ARTICHOKE
ASPARAGUS
BEETS
BROCCOLI
CABBAGE
CARROT
CAULIFLOWER
CELERY
GARLIC
GREEN PEAS
KALE
LETTUCE
ONION
POTATOES
SPINACH

ΑΓΚΙΝΑΡΑ
ΚΑΡΟΤΟ
ΠΡΑΣΙΝΑ ΜΠΙΖΕΛΙΑ
ΛΑΧΑΝΟ
ΜΠΡΟΚΟΛΟ
ΚΟΥΝΟΥΠΙΔΙ
ΠΑΤΑΤΕΣ
ΣΚΟΡΔΟ
ΣΠΑΝΑΚΙ
ΠΑΝΤΖΑΡΙΑ
ΜΑΡΟΥΛΙ
ΛΑΧΑΝΙΔΑ
ΣΕΛΙΝΟ
ΣΠΑΡΑΓΓΙΑ
ΚΡΕΜΜΥΔΙ

REVIEW: HOUSE

94

Review Jumble: The translations in the word list below have been scrambled. Draw lines between the left and right columns to find the correct translations.

B	D	C	Δ	I	A	M	E	P	I	Σ	M	A	Σ	Σ	B
E	N	L	A	B	T	I	A	H	Σ	K	E	Π	H	G	Δ
D	Y	E	A	A	A	A	Y	N	N	X	I	T	A	P	O
R	A	O	Y	W	H	S	B	E	N	T	X	R	O	Ά	E
O	P	I	F	E	N	C	E	E	I	A	A	M	D	B	Ю
O	A	E	P	O	H	M	O	M	P	G	A	Δ	R	E	Ω
M	M	Γ	K	A	P	A	Z	Φ	E	K	K	Γ	I	D	Ύ
O	A	O	O	N	Z	Ό	G	B	I	N	I	Д	V	I	C
O	K	Π	T	I	N	E	A	P	A	R	T	M	E	N	T
R	O	Y	R	Z	N	K	Π	Γ	A	T	C	N	W	I	T
G	T	O	P	Y	Θ	A	P	A	Π	T	H	F	A	N	E
N	A	F	E	O	C	A	Π	H	P	W	E	R	Y	G	E
I	B	A	Ώ	K	Σ	Q	H	M	D	T	N	E	O	R	F
V	E	E	T	I	N	O	Λ	A	Σ	W	I	N	D	O	W
I	P	L	Δ	Ά	G	S	Д	Θ	Я	U	A	W	O	O	M
L	K	I	A	X	I	Ώ	E	S	U	O	H	R	T	M	H

APARTMENT	ΔΙΑΜΕΡΙΣΜΑ
BASEMENT	ΥΠΟΓΕΙΟ
BATHROOM	ΤΡΑΠΕΖΑΡΙΑ
BED	ΚΟΥΖΙΝΑ
BEDROOM	ΜΠΑΝΙΟ
DINING ROOM	ΓΡΑΣΙΔΙ
DRIVEWAY	ΠΑΡΑΘΥΡΟ
FENCE	ΚΡΕΒΑΤΙ
GARAGE	ΣΚΕΠΗ
HOUSE	ΚΡΕΒΑΤΟΚΑΜΑΡΑ
KITCHEN	ΦΡΑΧΤΗΣ
LAWN	ΣΠΙΤΙ
LIVING ROOM	ΣΑΛΟΝΙ
ROOF	ΔΡΟΜΑΚΙ
WINDOW	ΓΚΑΡΑΖ

REVIEW: AROUND THE HOUSE 1

Review Time: Draw lines between the English word on the left and the corresponding translation on the right. Refer back to the original puzzle if you need help.

T	Σ	Ά	A	E	A	T	O	I	L	E	T	R	T	V	H
Σ	I	O	I	P	H	T	Ω	N	Γ	E	T	Σ	E	A	E
E	T	I	I	T	E	R	E	T	S	K	Z	P	S	C	W
Λ	S	P	X	A	Λ	I	E	Λ	V	R	M	S	A	U	A
A	F	H	A	W	Λ	P	P	I	A	A	I	L	B	U	S
K	M	T	N	Π	R	E	C	A	L	Y	P	A	U	M	H
Σ	O	N	R	A	E	D	Y	U	T	E	O	Δ	T	X	I
H	T	Y	C	E	K	Z	M	Λ	R	P	D	T	H	S	N
I	A	Λ	P	B	S	Π	I	I	O	T	Y	N	T	V	G
Π	B	Π	N	T	A	S	F	P	E	Π	A	Σ	A	P	M
I	L	J	A	N	I	Ύ	E	C	Ξ	B	E	I	B	H	A
Σ	E	Ω	I	Λ	K	N	U	R	P	Π	C	H	N	E	C
I	T	E	A	H	D	A	A	Y	D	R	Y	E	R	E	H
N	P	M	I	J	F	K	Σ	P	T	Z	A	K	I	O	I
A	Π	Y	O	K	Σ	H	K	I	P	T	K	E	Λ	H	N
A	M	S	W	I	M	M	I	N	G	P	O	O	L	N	E

BATHTUB	ΜΠΑΝΙΕΡΑ
CARPET	ΠΙΣΙΝΑ
CHANDELIER	ΚΟΥΡΤΙΝΑ
CURTAIN	ΤΖΑΚΙ
DRESSER	ΠΟΛΥΕΛΑΙΟΣ
DRYER	ΠΛΥΝΤΗΡΙΟ
FAUCET	ΣΥΡΤΑΡΙΕΡΑ
FIREPLACE	ΗΛΕΚΤΡΙΚΗ ΣΚΟΥΠΑ
LAMP	ΒΡΥΣΗ
SWIMMING POOL	ΤΟΥΑΛΕΤΑ
STAIRS	ΧΑΛΙ
TABLE	ΤΡΑΠΕΖΙ
TOILET	ΣΤΕΓΝΩΤΗΡΙΟ
VACUUM	ΣΚΑΛΕΣ
WASHING MACHINE	ΛΑΜΠΑ

REVIEW: AROUND THE HOUSE 2

Review Jumble: The translations in the word list below have been scrambled. Draw lines between the left and right columns to find the correct translations.

N R E F R I G E R A T O R A Y M N
E T O P Ψ Y Γ E I O V B N E Z S Ω
A Ψ O R S H A M U E I K N I S U T
H Λ Я Y R E H A N R E M I E W Y A
A Θ K A Λ I Ю Ξ C E I D R N A S I
N E P E Ί A M I B H E T S W G Σ Π
T N A A P A Π Λ C S T H L T P L O
K A M I N A Δ A K A O L P E Y T I
A N Ω N P I K P M W A A M S T K P
Θ E P Y P Q O I E H E H N O T O H
P P T O Ά A T R R S P I L L O W T
E O Σ K N A F G N I L I E C Y O N
Φ X O Λ T Ξ A Σ M D A R O K S E Y
T Y T R Z T Я X Y P P H A A Д O Λ
H T O Ά Ψ N E N K O Z E C R Ό T Π
Σ H Φ O P O Σ A P H T Σ I M E N A
Ξ Σ O N P Y O Φ E Λ Y N Ψ E X Y Γ

CHAIR	ΘΡΑΝΙΟ
CEILING FAN	ΚΑΜΙΝΑΔΑ
CHIMNEY	ΝΕΡΟΧΥΤΗΣ
CLOSET	ΚΑΡΕΚΛΑ
CRIB	ΣΤΡΩΜΑ
DESK	ΦΟΥΡΝΟΣ
DISHWASHER	ΑΝΕΜΙΣΤΗΡΑΣ ΟΡΟΦΗΣ
HALLWAY	ΠΛΥΝΤΗΡΙΟ ΠΙΑΤΩΝ
MATTRESS	ΝΤΟΥΣ
MIRROR	ΜΑΞΙΛΑΡΙ
OVEN	ΝΤΟΥΛΑΠΑ
PILLOW	ΚΟΥΝΙΑ
REFRIGERATOR	ΨΥΓΕΙΟ
SHOWER	ΧΟΛ
SINK	ΚΑΘΡΕΦΤΗΣ

REVIEW: AT THE TABLE

Review Time: Draw lines between the English word on the left and the corresponding translation on the right. Refer back to the original puzzle if you need help.

K	N	I	T	A	R	E	H	C	T	I	P	S	S	I	K
K	O	R	Σ	Φ	Λ	O	Π	M	I	Λ	A	T	Y	O	K
Y	F	Y	Ί	A	Y	A	K	R	O	F	O	A	Y	O	O
Я	T	Д	T	P	P	E	T	T	I	T	S	T	Y	Λ	Π
X	Я	A	E	A	Ά	K	E	I	A	X	A	Π	H	I	E
O	A	Y	B	K	Λ	K	A	B	L	Λ	A	T	Π	T	T
N	N	P	R	L	E	I	L	I	I	Ά	N	E	E	P	R
I	O	B	T	T	E	E	T	T	Γ	A	P	E	F	W	I
K	O	O	H	O	C	S	O	H	M	I	N	F	I	Ξ	N
P	P	W	P	L	Π	Y	P	O	Σ	P	P	N	N	U	Y
A	S	L	O	S	Γ	E	Z	O	L	Σ	E	H	K	E	O
N	B	T	S	Λ	A	E	T	A	O	G	O	P	T	X	P
S	H	A	Y	E	Π	E	T	Σ	L	N	U	Y	P	O	H
R	L	K	Λ	A	R	E	T	A	E	E	N	M	Π	E	Π
G	O	H	P	T	L	A	S	Π	O	T	H	P	I	A	R
Y	O	T	A	I	Π	S	P	I	P	I	A	X	A	M	Σ

BOWL
FORK
GLASS
KNIFE
MUG
NAPKIN
PEPPER
PITCHER
PLATE
SALT
SPOON
TABLECLOTH
TABLESPOON
TEASPOON
WINE GLASS

ΜΑΧΑΙΡΙ
ΠΙΠΕΡΙ
ΚΟΥΠΑ
ΠΗΡΟΥΝΙ
ΜΠΟΛ
ΠΟΤΗΡΙ ΓΙΑ ΚΡΑΣΙ
ΚΟΥΤΑΛΙ ΤΗΣ ΣΟΥΠΑΣ
ΚΟΥΤΑΛΙ ΤΟΥ ΓΛΥΚΟΥ
ΠΙΑΤΟ
ΧΑΡΤΟΠΕΤΣΕΤΑ
ΚΟΥΤΑΛΙ
ΚΑΡΑΦΑ
ΑΛΑΤΙ
ΠΟΤΗΡΙ
ΤΡΑΠΕΖΟΜΑΝΤΗΛΟ

REVIEW: TOOLS

98

Review Jumble: The translations in the word list below have been scrambled. Draw lines between the left and right columns to find the correct translations.

Ю	X	R	E	H	S	A	W	R	E	N	C	H	Я	T
I	P	R	E	V	I	R	D	W	E	R	C	S	I	A
Δ	E	Ю	T	M	E	W	E	R	C	S	I	N	Δ	P
I	N	U	T	D	M	L	L	I	R	D	O	X	I	E
B	C	S	D	T	Λ	A	B	O	L	Λ	Ώ	M	E	M
A	I	A	Ύ	K	P	B	H	M	Y	P	M	Γ	Λ	E
Σ	L	W	O	A	H	Y	I	O	C	B	O	Ω	K	A
T	E	E	M	P	H	N	Π	Δ	A	Y	Λ	Ю	O	S
A	V	U	B	Φ	O	M	I	A	A	T	Y	Ю	K	U
K	E	O	N	I	T	P	Λ	Ю	N	M	B	A	I	R
N	L	S	P	N	Y	E	T	Ύ	Ί	I	I	Δ	Λ	E
T	I	Π	K	Φ	Δ	E	Π	E	N	Σ	A	Ξ	Λ	E
Γ	A	Ω	Σ	O	P	B	I	R	M	Φ	I	Ό	A	Ύ
B	N	W	P	M	S	B	T	Ώ	Λ	E	N	E	Γ	Π
I	R	Θ	D	I	H	A	Λ	A	K	Σ	E	X	Π	Ώ

BOLT	ΓΑΛΛΙΚΟ ΚΛΕΙΔΙ
DRILL	ΠΑΞΙΜΑΔΙ
HAMMER	ΡΟΔΕΛΑ
LADDER	ΜΕΤΡΟ
LEVEL	ΒΙΔΑ
NAIL	ΜΟΛΥΒΙ
NUT	ΜΠΟΥΛΟΝΙ
PENCIL	ΤΡΥΠΑΝΙ
PLIERS	ΠΕΝΣΑ
SAW	ΠΡΙΟΝΙ
SCREW	ΚΑΤΣΑΒΙΔΙ
SCREWDRIVER	ΑΛΦΑΔΙ
TAPE MEASURE	ΣΦΥΡΙ
WASHER	ΣΚΑΛΑ
WRENCH	ΚΑΡΦΙ

REVIEW: CLOTHES 1

Review Time: Draw lines between the English word on the left and the corresponding translation on the right. Refer back to the original puzzle if you need help.

```
S P F D Φ Σ D J G O S M O M E
Ψ B O R K P T R T Ί E I Λ Π N
L P A J A M A S E V O L G O O
S E I T K C E N A S H A C Y A
W O A B H V S I T H S I Y P Σ
E H E P Λ R Σ Π Y S N T H N Q
A L E E O T O O Y O B N A O O
T Γ F B Y M F B Λ T Ω A H Y Ά
E T I O Ί A I E E Z Z Γ K Z Σ
R Π Π Λ B S T T Ύ U F A N I T
A A S Y E N K A Π E Λ O M M P
Π Λ Φ O A K E Ω B T Δ H O E O
B T Z Π N Λ O K Σ A K Λ Θ Z Σ
A O S K C O S E Φ O P E M A J
S T R O H S Σ T A O C Γ A P Ω
```

BATHROBE
BELT
COAT
DRESS
GLOVES
HAT
NECKTIE
PAJAMAS
PANTS
SCARF
SHOES
SHORTS
SOCKS
SWEATER
VEST

ΚΑΠΕΛΟ
ΠΥΤΖΑΜΕΣ
ΜΠΟΥΡΝΟΥΖΙ
ΠΑΠΟΥΤΣΙΑ
ΠΑΝΤΕΛΟΝΙ
ΣΟΡΤΣ
ΖΩΝΗ
ΓΡΑΒΑΤΑ
ΚΑΛΤΣΕΣ
ΓΙΛΕΚΟ
ΠΑΛΤΟ
ΓΑΝΤΙΑ
ΠΟΥΛΟΒΕΡ
ΦΟΡΕΜΑ
ΚΑΣΚΟΛ

REVIEW: CLOTHES 2

Review Jumble: The translations in the word list below have been scrambled. Draw lines between the left and right columns to find the correct translations.

```
T K D L Q Φ A Π O Y K A M I Σ O
H A O T I P A N T E Σ O B L Ά S
B Ώ M Λ O Π Д M Q S T G R S C T
H P M Y I E W R I S T W A T C H
A I A Γ Δ E Σ M O W S S C O A S
Ώ Δ I X E N S Ω O Φ K U E O H I
P O Λ O I X E I P O Σ I L B N S
N U A Σ M O Γ I Y O T T E N C A
H N Δ E O A Λ Σ T W Y C T L H N
Z D N T M C T I O Y A X O A L D
T E A O B O S B V L O T O B R A
Z R Σ Π Y Y N O K H H Σ R B Λ L
F W E M P O A C T I U S M I W S
E E I X S R E D N E P S U S K E
M A X E H N J G B N B H Ί H O S
T R I H S E Φ O Y Σ T A A A R O
```

WRIST WATCH	TZHN
BOOTS	ΚΟΛΙΕ
BOW TIE	ΠΟΥΚΑΜΙΣΟ
BRA	ΠΑΠΙΓΙΟΝ
BRACELET	ΡΟΛΟΙ ΧΕΙΡΟΣ
CLOTHING	ΣΑΝΔΑΛΙΑ
JEANS	ΤΙΡΑΝΤΕΣ
NECKLACE	ΣΟΥΤΙΕΝ
SANDALS	ΒΡΑΧΙΟΛΙ
SHIRT	ΜΠΟΤΕΣ
SKIRT	ΜΑΓΙΟ
SUIT	ΚΟΥΣΤΟΥΜΙ
SUSPENDERS	ΕΝΔΥΜΑ
SWIM SUIT	ΕΣΩΡΟΥΧΟ
UNDERWEAR	ΦΟΥΣΤΑ

REVIEW: GETTING READY

101

Review Time: Draw lines between the English word on the left and the corresponding translation on the right. Refer back to the original puzzle if you need help.

Β	Α	Ι	Σ	Α	Π	Ο	Υ	Ν	Ι	Κ	Α	Φ	Α	Ρ	Υ	Ξ
M	E	H	P	M	E	S	N	M	E	M	U	F	R	E	P	Φ
O	F	H	T	O	O	T	H	P	A	S	T	E	N	B	Ю	A
C	D	D	D	O	T	U	A	A	S	K	Y	P	O	P	Ώ	K
O	O	E	E	Ψ	O	O	T	B	M	R	E	Δ	T	E	Я	O
N	O	N	O	N	S	T	X	H	D	P	O	U	H	N	Δ	I
T	Δ	T	D	Σ	A	T	H	R	W	N	O	K	P	O	Ί	E
A	O	A	O	I	E	Π	I	B	T	A	C	O	N	I	A	Π
C	N	L	R	N	T	A	O	O	R	I	S	T	N	Σ	H	A
T	T	F	A	A	H	I	B	Σ	T	U	I	H	O	I	C	Φ
L	O	L	N	B	Z	O	O	S	M	K	S	A	I	T	O	H
E	K	O	T	J	Y	O	P	N	O	H	T	H	Γ	N	U	Σ
N	P	S	M	P	A	I	R	N	E	O	T	E	A	O	Π	V
S	E	S	T	P	L	H	H	Y	X	R	L	I	P	K	J	E
E	M	Σ	Ω	Σ	A	M	Π	O	Y	A	N	A	K	N	O	Ώ
S	A	M	Y	Λ	A	I	Δ	O	K	I	T	A	M	O	T	Σ
Ω	A	M	E	I	K	A	Π	I	Σ	T	O	Λ	A	K	I	T

COMB	ΣΤΟΜΑΤΙΚΟ ΔΙΑΛΥΜΑ
CONDITIONER	ΚΡΑΓΙΟΝ
CONTACT LENSES	ΦΑΚΟΙ ΕΠΑΦΗΣ
DENTAL FLOSS	ΣΑΜΠΟΥΑΝ
DEODORANT	ΧΤΕΝΑ
HAIR DRYER	ΣΑΠΟΥΝΙ
LIPSTICK	ΞΥΡΑΦΑΚΙ
MAKEUP	ΟΔΟΝΤΟΒΟΥΡΤΣΑ
MOUTHWASH	ΜΕΙΚΑΠ
PERFUME	ΟΔΟΝΤΙΚΟ ΝΗΜΑ
RAZOR	ΟΔΟΝΤΟΚΡΕΜΑ
SHAMPOO	ΑΠΟΣΜΗΤΙΚΟ
SOAP	ΠΙΣΤΟΛΑΚΙ
TOOTHBRUSH	ΑΡΩΜΑ
TOOTHPASTE	ΚΟΝΤΙΣΙΟΝΕΡ

REVIEW: PLACES 1

Review Jumble: The translations in the word list below have been scrambled. Draw lines between the left and right columns to find the correct translations.

```
U Σ T A Δ I O I E M O K O Σ O N H
P O Σ Ψ H K I T Σ E B Σ O P Y Π H
F K I O L N Θ Γ O M O Y Σ E I O Ί
S I E E P I P L E O Π A O E I C E
N M F T M A R Δ A E M U S E U M Π
O O T I Φ O Φ V P T S R T C L Γ O
I P K E R A P M L U I J A I I E Λ
T Δ I X P E A Δ P O O P G F T Φ Y
A O N M B P S E Y I O H S F V Y K
T P A K K A R T E X T H C O Z P A
S H P E V M R Λ A H A M C T H A T
N Δ T N A O O B O T U T E S Ю R A
I I E R P X R U G I I U E O Σ P Σ
A Σ K R Σ I S E D Ξ Y O P P H L T
R E I N D E P A R T M E N T W C H
T A H G A Γ T O F F I C E P A Π M
H B E O R S V O I M O P Δ O P E A
```

AIRPORT	ΣΤΑΔΙΟ
BAR	ΤΑΧΥΔΡΟΜΕΙΟ
BRIDGE	ΣΙΔΗΡΟΔΡΟΜΙΚΟΣ σταθμοσ
DEPARTMENT store	ΓΡΑΦΕΙΟ
FARM	ΑΕΡΟΔΡΟΜΙΟ
FIRE STATION	ΜΠΑΡ
HOSPITAL	ΠΥΡΟΣΒΕΣΤΙΚΗ
LIGHTHOUSE	ΦΑΡΟΣ
MUSEUM	ΝΟΣΟΚΟΜΕΙΟ
OFFICE	ΣΧΟΛΕΙΟ
POST OFFICE	ΣΟΥΠΕΡΜΑΡΚΕΤ
SCHOOL	ΓΕΦΥΡΑ
STADIUM	ΦΑΡΜΑ
SUPERMARKET	ΜΟΥΣΕΙΟ
TRAIN STATION	ΠΟΛΥΚΑΤΑΣΤΗΜΑ

REVIEW: PLACES 2

Review Time: Draw lines between the English word on the left and the corresponding translation on the right. Refer back to the original puzzle if you need help.

P N H N T E A A I Σ Ξ R Z C T R Ά
Ό B O P E R A H O U S E A Π A A Y
Ό D T I O I H R O Д U S A T Σ R C
Z R E S T A U R A N T N H T E O A
T N L Y R A R B I L E E Y T F T M
E H E B Д Д T V E Π A N E F P E R
I Φ O K Φ L E S I T O M E A H Σ A
A R A A P R K Σ E M E E R B K T H
M Z M P S O T R I C S K O A H I P
H W E I M H T K Ψ H I Ю T N Θ A Ό
T O T Π M A O A O A I L S K O T Y
Σ Y K I A T K P Φ M Д N O A I O A
A O O A M P P E E E Δ O A P Λ P O
T K E H Σ K T Ξ I Σ I B Ό M B I V
A P M T A T Ξ E N O Δ O X E I O A
K A Φ E T E P I A A F G T B B Λ O
A Π Д A P E Π O P T A E Θ P S Я O

BANK	ΤΡΑΠΕΖΑ
CASTLE	ΚΑΦΕΤΕΡΙΑ
CEMETERY	ΦΑΡΜΑΚΕΙΟ
COFFEE SHOP	ΟΠΕΡΑ
HARBOR	ΞΕΝΟΔΟΧΕΙΟ
HOTEL	ΝΕΚΡΟΤΑΦΕΙΟ
LIBRARY	ΑΣΤΥΝΟΜΙΚΟ ΤΜΗΜΑ
OPERA HOUSE	ΚΑΤΑΣΤΗΜΑ
PARK	ΛΙΜΑΝΙ
PHARMACY	ΠΑΝΕΠΙΣΤΗΜΙΟ
POLICE STATION	ΠΑΡΚΟ
RESTAURANT	ΚΑΣΤΡΟ
STORE	ΒΙΒΛΙΟΘΗΚΗ
THEATER	ΘΕΑΤΡΟ
UNIVERSITY	ΕΣΤΙΑΤΟΡΙΟ

REVIEW: ON THE ROAD

Review Jumble: The translations in the word list below have been scrambled. Draw lines between the left and right columns to find the correct translations.

Σ	T	O	T	H	N	I	K	O	T	Y	A	T	O	Π	Ί	B
A	T	Y	X	H	M	A	G	I	E	M	E	Ψ	I	U	Z	Ά
Δ	B	A	O	Z	Θ	P	Π	L	N	E	E	N	W	C	H	A
I	W	E	Y	I	O	T	C	A	R	H	A	T	Ψ	M	Σ	N
P	T	M	N	T	E	Y	K	T	P	K	Σ	K	Δ	O	O	G
Ω	B	R	S	Z	C	P	S	Λ	I	K	C	H	M	T	M	I
Λ	A	S	A	R	I	Y	O	Δ	E	U	I	O	O	O	O	S
T	U	E	O	F	A	N	A	Φ	R	Ω	P	N	Γ	Σ	P	P
B	T	T	N	W	F	Σ	A	T	Ω	Δ	Φ	H	Γ	Y	Δ	O
O	O	T	E	A	T	I	R	Δ	O	E	T	O	B	K	Z	T
M	M	N	D	O	L	A	C	N	I	P	Λ	H	P	Λ	Δ	S
M	O	E	Π	A	F	V	O	L	O	K	Y	H	M	E	I	U
H	B	D	E	F	O	M	X	Φ	I	T	O	Θ	Σ	T	I	B
O	I	I	I	P	A	R	K	I	N	G	L	O	T	A	Ό	O
E	L	C	B	E	N	Z	I	N	H	Ό	H	Ξ	P	Ύ	T	Θ
O	E	C	H	X	A	G	A	S	S	T	A	T	I	O	N	Σ
Ώ	G	A	S	O	L	I	N	E	Φ	A	N	A	P	I	O	A

AUTOMOBILE	ΛΩΡΙΔΑ
ACCIDENT	ΔΡΟΜΟΣ
BUS	ΦΟΡΤΗΓΟ
BUS STOP	ΒΕΝΖΙΝΑΔΙΚΟ
GAS STATION	ΜΟΝΟΔΡΟΜΟΣ
GASOLINE	ΠΑΡΚΙΝΓΚ
LANE	ΑΤΥΧΗΜΑ
MOTORCYCLE	ΦΑΝΑΡΙ
ONE-WAY STREET	ΛΕΩΦΟΡΕΙΟ
PARKING LOT	ΒΕΝΖΙΝΗ
ROAD	ΚΙΝΗΣΗ
STOP SIGN	ΠΙΝΑΚΙΔΑ ΣΤΟΠ
TRAFFIC LIGHT	ΜΟΤΟΣΥΚΛΕΤΑ
TRAFFIC	ΣΤΑΣΗ ΛΕΩΦΟΡΕΙΟΥ
TRUCK	ΑΥΤΟΚΙΝΗΤΟ

REVIEW: GETTING AROUND

Review Time: Draw lines between the English word on the left and the corresponding translation on the right. Refer back to the original puzzle if you need help.

Π	Ο	Δ	Η	Λ	Α	Τ	Ο	Π	Μ	Ι	Ρ	Ε	Φ	Η	Γ	Π
Ρ	Ώ	Ι	Я	Ο	Ι	Χ	Υ	Ρ	Β	Ο	Π	Υ	Ο	Τ	Υ	Σ
F	Ρ	Τ	Ε	Ο	Α	Χ	F	Κ	Ε	Λ	Ύ	V	Α	Ρ	Κ	Ύ
Χ	Ο	Β	Ε	Ρ	Κ	Ρ	Α	Φ	Τ	Τ	Ε	Μ	Ο	Α	W	Ε
Θ	S	F	Ε	Β	Ο	Ν	S	S	Μ	R	Π	Σ	Φ	Σ	Α	Ι
Ν	C	Ι	C	Ο	Ο	Φ	Ν	U	C	Τ	Β	Ο	Ο	C	Π	S
Ι	Η	R	Ν	Τ	Ρ	Π	Ω	R	Β	Ε	Σ	Μ	Κ	Ε	Ο	Ε
Ρ	Ο	Ε	Α	R	Д	Ο	Α	Ε	Σ	Μ	Ο	Κ	Ρ	Ι	R	Τ
Ο	Ο	Τ	L	Α	Υ	F	Φ	Τ	Λ	Ρ	Α	Ι	Ν	Α	Λ	Ρ
Ν	L	R	U	Ι	Τ	Ο	Ι	Ο	Δ	Ο	Π	R	C	Α	Α	Ε
Α	Β	U	Β	Ν	C	Κ	Β	Ο	Ν	Ο	Κ	Ε	Ι	Ύ	Τ	Ν
Λ	U	C	Μ	S	Ο	Ο	Ρ	Ι	Λ	Ε	C	Ι	Τ	Ν	Ο	Ο
Π	S	Κ	Α	Ο	U	Η	Ρ	Ι	C	Ι	Θ	Ο	Λ	Ε	Ε	Ε
Ο	Ί	L	Χ	Χ	Δ	Β	Κ	Τ	L	Υ	Κ	Σ	Ν	Ο	Ο	L
Ρ	Χ	Η	Ρ	Ι	Ο	Ο	W	Ο	Ε	Δ	C	Ν	Α	Ν	Χ	Ψ
Ε	Μ	Ν	Σ	Α	Τ	Τ	Ρ	Α	Ι	R	Ρ	L	Α	Ν	Ε	Σ
Α	Ο	L	Τ	Τ	F	Ε	R	R	Υ	Η	Μ	C	Ε	Τ	Α	Η

AIRPLANE	ΑΣΘΕΝΟΦΟΡΟ
AMBULANCE	ΣΧΟΛΙΚΟ ΛΕΩΦΟΡΕΙΟ
BICYCLE	ΤΡΕΝΟ
BOAT	ΣΚΑΦΟΣ
CANOE	ΑΕΡΟΠΛΑΝΟ
FERRY	ΠΕΡΙΠΟΛΙΚΟ
FIRE TRUCK	ΕΛΙΚΟΠΤΕΡΟ
HELICOPTER	ΠΥΡΟΣΒΕΣΤΙΚΟ ΟΧΗΜΑ
HOVERCRAFT	υπογειοσ ΣΙΔΗΡΟΔΡΟΜΟΣ
POLICE CAR	ΤΑΝΚΣ
SCHOOL BUS	ΠΟΔΗΛΑΤΟ
SUBMARINE	ΚΑΝΟ
SUBWAY	ΧΟΒΕΡΚΡΑΦΤ
TANK	ΦΕΡΙΜΠΟΤ
TRAIN	ΥΠΟΒΡΥΧΙΟ

REVIEW: LANGUAGES 1

Review Jumble: The translations in the word list below have been scrambled. Draw lines between the left and right columns to find the correct translations.

B	G	E	R	M	A	N	H	W	P	O	L	I	S	H	Z
P	R	U	S	S	I	A	N	A	E	R	O	K	A	R	T
Γ	H	C	N	E	R	F	P	A	K	R	P	R	B	E	P
A	T	Ξ	A	A	M	P	Γ	O	K	O	B	I	T	M	H
Λ	G	A	B	K	Ω	A	P	E	R	I	A	E	A	O	Π
Λ	D	I	K	Σ	I	E	N	T	P	Π	N	N	H	N	O
I	C	R	I	I	A	Z	U	T	Ω	M	Δ	A	I	A	Λ
K	J	K	X	T	Λ	G	E	N	E	A	A	R	Π	M	Ω
A	A	A	I	S	U	A	E	M	P	I	A	N	I	Σ	N
K	P	K	P	E	P	Z	Γ	I	A	D	V	T	I	A	I
I	A	K	S	A	I	A	N	O	N	N	A	I	T	K	K
N	B	E	E	K	N	I	N	A	T	L	T	X	A	X	A
H	I	T	A	E	K	E	M	I	I	P	T	E	Λ	Ψ	Φ
Λ	K	Y	E	A	R	T	S	A	S	S	O	S	I	Φ	L
Λ	A	H	S	I	L	G	N	E	D	H	K	Π	K	B	O
E	B	P	A	I	K	A	A	Γ	Γ	Λ	I	K	A	E	Ά

ARABIC	ΑΡΑΒΙΚΑ
ENGLISH	ΠΟΛΩΝΙΚΑ
FRENCH	ΜΑΝΔΑΡΙΝΙΚΑ
GERMAN	ΒΙΕΤΝΑΜΕΖΙΚΑ
GREEK	ΙΤΑΛΙΚΑ
ITALIAN	ΓΕΡΜΑΝΙΚΑ
JAPANESE	ΚΟΡΕΑΤΙΚΑ
KOREAN	ΡΩΣΙΚΑ
MANDARIN	ΙΣΠΑΝΙΚΑ
POLISH	ΓΑΛΛΙΚΑ
PORTUGUESE	ΕΛΛΗΝΙΚΑ
RUSSIAN	ΕΒΡΑΙΚΑ
SPANISH	ΙΑΠΩΝΕΖΙΚΑ
HEBREW	ΑΓΓΛΙΚΑ
VIETNAMESE	ΠΟΡΤΟΓΑΛΙΚΑ

REVIEW: PROFESSIONS

Review Time: Draw lines between the English word on the left and the corresponding translation on the right. Refer back to the original puzzle if you need help.

P I L O T C E T I H C R A L Я N R
P S Ύ Σ U F Δ L R I E H A L M Π E
Σ I Ξ S O Д I O E T A W E H N T H
O O Y O X P T R N C Y H X F N P C
I E Λ H A C O E E E T A T E Z S A
O Ψ O A O P P Γ R F N R O O E Y E
Π O Y D K R X H H I I Δ I I N C T
O Ю P X A Σ Γ I K K O G I C G H S
Θ W Γ C I I A O T N I M H E I I I
H Π O K A A Σ Δ T E A Δ A T N A T
Θ I Σ T U T T I S D K Φ N A E T N
Ώ Λ P Ω Ω Ю A P T T Ψ T E U E R E
F O T A Σ T Y N O M I K O Σ R I D
Σ T Π Y P O Σ B E Σ T H Σ N A S S
Д O Σ O M O K O Σ O N Π G H A T E
Σ Σ Σ I H Λ E K T P O Λ O Γ O Σ A
P O L I C E O F F I C E R O T C A

ACTOR	ΑΣΤΥΝΟΜΙΚΟΣ
ARCHITECT	ΔΑΣΚΑΛΟΣ
CARPENTER	ΗΛΕΚΤΡΟΛΟΓΟΣ
CHEF	ΠΙΛΟΤΟΣ
DENTIST	ΣΕΦ
DOCTOR	ΟΔΟΝΤΙΑΤΡΟΣ
ELECTRICIAN	ΓΙΑΤΡΟΣ
ENGINEER	ΨΥΧΙΑΤΡΟΣ
FIRE FIGHTER	ΝΟΣΟΚΟΜΟΣ
LAWYER	ΔΙΚΗΓΟΡΟΣ
NURSE	ΜΗΧΑΝΙΚΟΣ
PILOT	ΗΘΟΠΟΙΟΣ
POLICE OFFICER	ΞΥΛΟΥΡΓΟΣ
PSYCHIATRIST	ΑΡΧΙΤΕΚΤΟΝΑΣ
TEACHER	ΠΥΡΟΣΒΕΣΤΗΣ

REVIEW: PROFESSIONS 2

Review Jumble: The translations in the word list below have been scrambled. Draw lines between the left and right columns to find the correct translations.

Z Σ A N O M H T Σ I Π E P Φ H T W
T O R R Σ H Λ Ω Π O Θ N A Ά L Σ Σ
Ό K B O I E M Γ X E K P A Φ T H Σ
Δ I A Σ Ω Σ T H Σ O F I P L Π T B
Σ Λ T I H T O O X L P O T M Y Ω U
H Y O Σ Y T A K O A L E E I E M K
N A P Ύ H A H R I I N C Y B Λ M S
X P R A R T I Γ T Σ H I U T Ά O A
E Δ O C R S Σ I H A Y T K Γ H K Π
T Y F C T A C I N Θ C O Ύ O H Σ M
I R E O A I M I Γ H A E M E Σ U Σ
Λ E S U A M C E E O R K E I S H H
Λ B S N L E D R D N Λ E Λ I Π C T
A M O T A I L O R I T I C A A P H
K U R A R T I S T Θ C I Σ N N E Λ
A L A N R E B R A B A A S K A E Θ
K P A T H L E T E N X Ό H T E D A

ACCOUNTANT	ΥΔΡΑΥΛΙΚΟΣ
ARTIST	ΠΟΛΙΤΙΚΟΣ
ATHLETE	ΑΝΘΟΠΩΛΗΣ
BARBER	ΚΟΜΜΩΤΗΣ
BUTCHER	ΜΟΥΣΙΚΟΣ
DANCER	ΔΙΑΣΩΣΤΗΣ
FLORIST	ΜΗΧΑΝΙΚΟΣ
MECHANIC	ΡΑΦΤΗΣ
MUSICIAN	ΕΠΙΣΤΗΜΟΝΑΣ
PARAMEDIC	ΚΑΛΛΙΤΕΧΝΗΣ
PLUMBER	ΑΘΛΗΤΗΣ
POLITICIAN	ΛΟΓΙΣΤΗΣ
PROFESSOR	ΧΟΡΕΥΤΗΣ
SCIENTIST	ΧΑΣΑΠΗΣ
TAILOR	ΚΑΘΗΓΗΤΗΣ

REVIEW: PROFESSIONS 3

Review Time: Draw lines between the English word on the left and the corresponding translation on the right. Refer back to the original puzzle if you need help.

M Γ R E V I R D I X A T Ί Δ Y Y Ί
Π Σ Δ O R E N E D R A G H Ό O Z Φ
A H H P T Y T R D R E M Z I O A M
P T L Λ D A P E E N O L E O P Ό A
M Σ K L Ω Θ L I R Σ E P E M Φ F I
A A F Ώ I Π D S I I O T A W I T L
N P I D B L O O N Φ N K R S E A C
T Φ Ξ F O U Γ T Ω A O A H A Γ J A
A A A S A P S E A Π R E R P B O R
X T T S A R Λ D O M R T O I Ψ U R
Y E Σ Φ Γ Σ M I R M H T K A A R I
Δ M O A O X O E A I H M P Π S N E
P Σ Γ Γ T Σ P N R Σ V A Σ H W A R
O Σ H T Ω I T A P T Σ E O O W L B
M Δ Δ I K H Π O Y P O Σ R I K I H
O Σ O P T A I N H T K A Π N M S T
Σ T S Ί X H P H A R M A C I S T V

BARTENDER	ΜΕΤΑΦΡΑΣΤΗΣ
BUS DRIVER	ΤΑΧΥΔΡΟΜΟΣ
FARMER	ΨΑΡΑΣ
FISHERMAN	ΜΠΑΡΜΑΝ
GARDENER	ΦΑΡΜΑΚΟΠΟΙΟΣ
JEWELER	ΚΗΠΟΥΡΟΣ
JOURNALIST	ΣΤΡΑΤΙΩΤΗΣ
MAIL CARRIER	ΟΔΗΓΟΣ ΤΑΞΙ
PHARMACIST	ΟΔΗΓΟΣ ΛΕΩΦΟΡΕΙΟΥ
SOLDIER	ΚΟΣΜΗΜΑΤΟΠΩΛΗΣ
TAXI DRIVER	ΚΤΗΝΙΑΤΡΟΣ
TRANSLATOR	ΔΗΜΟΣΙΟΓΡΑΦΟΣ
VETERINARIAN	ΑΓΡΟΤΗΣ

REVIEW: SOLAR SYSTEM

110

Review Jumble: The translations in the word list below have been scrambled. Draw lines between the left and right columns to find the correct translations.

Η	Λ	Ι	Α	Κ	Ο	Σ	Υ	Σ	Τ	Η	Μ	Α	Χ	D
Σ	Η	Δ	Ι	Ε	Ο	Ρ	Ε	Τ	Σ	Α	Λ	Β	Η	A
O	H	T	I	Δ	O	P	Φ	A	O	H	Ώ	I	U	P
N	O	C	E	Ώ	M	Ύ	N	Σ	N	Λ	X	J	O	H
A	C	O	Δ	H	Φ	Ω	A	Δ	O	M	A	R	S	Σ
P	L	M	Σ	K	T	E	D	H	P	N	N	Φ	O	V
Y	H	E	D	Y	O	E	Γ	I	K	O	K	M	L	E
O	E	T	O	Φ	O	M	A	Γ	O	P	E	E	A	N
T	Z	Λ	R	Y	S	P	H	M	A	R	E	R	R	U
A	Π	C	R	A	T	E	R	T	C	P	E	E	S	S
E	N	U	T	P	E	N	H	U	H	Σ	I	T	Y	U
P	L	U	T	O	T	P	R	Γ	A	Σ	I	I	S	N
N	R	J	S	Φ	A	Y	O	I	T	T	L	P	T	A
N	O	Π	O	Σ	E	I	Δ	Ω	N	A	Σ	U	E	R
O	M	I	E	P	D	F	O	E	T	T	O	J	M	U

SOLAR SYSTEM	ΠΟΣΕΙΔΩΝΑΣ
MERCURY	ΕΡΜΗΣ
VENUS	ΔΙΑΣ
EARTH	ΟΥΡΑΝΟΣ
MOON	ΗΛΙΑΚΟ ΣΥΣΤΗΜΑ
MARS	ΑΦΡΟΔΙΤΗ
JUPITER	ΑΣΤΕΡΟΕΙΔΗΣ
SATURN	ΗΛΙΟΣ
URANUS	ΓΗ
NEPTUNE	ΠΛΟΥΤΩΝΑΣ
PLUTO	ΚΡΟΝΟΣ
SUN	ΚΟΜΗΤΗΣ
CRATER	ΑΡΗΣ
ASTEROID	ΦΕΓΓΑΡΙ
COMET	ΚΡΑΤΗΡΑΣ

REVIEW: MUSICAL INSTRUMENTS 111

Review Time: Draw lines between the English word on the left and the corresponding translation on the right. Refer back to the original puzzle if you need help.

Q	N	E	N	O	B	M	O	R	T	Q	H	H	W	B
G	A	G	U	I	T	A	R	D	M	A	Ώ	Ю	K	T
N	M	Γ	Γ	T	H	A	G	X	R	O	P	I	R	I
S	T	K	A	P	Π	A	K	P	P	U	Θ	U	Φ	Φ
Я	Σ	A	Ξ	O	Φ	Ω	N	O	I	A	M	E	A	Y
Ώ	M	I	E	M	Λ	I	B	W	P	P	T	S	T	Σ
Ю	A	N	G	Π	A	N	D	A	E	N	E	Ω	E	A
P	P	T	I	O	O	O	I	T	O	N	T	S	Π	P
I	T	A	Ύ	N	Y	I	Ю	L	O	Λ	M	E	M	M
Λ	N	Д	R	I	T	D	A	H	O	N	E	R	O	O
O	F	T	E	P	O	R	P	D	B	I	A	Σ	P	N
I	L	H	A	R	M	O	N	I	C	A	V	I	T	I
B	U	N	E	N	X	C	E	L	L	O	Σ	Q	P	K
D	T	U	B	A	A	C	H	E	T	O	Y	M	Π	A
L	E	A	S	A	T	A	M	B	O	U	R	I	N	E

ACCORDION
BAGPIPES
CELLO
DRUMS
FLUTE
GUITAR
HARMONICA
HARP
PIANO
SAXOPHONE
TAMBOURINE
TROMBONE
TRUMPET
TUBA
VIOLIN

ΤΡΟΜΠΕΤΑ
ΑΡΠΑ
ΤΟΥΜΠΑ
ΣΑΞΟΦΩΝΟ
ΦΛΑΟΥΤΟ
ΝΤΡΑΜΣ
ΓΚΑΙΝΤΑ
ΒΙΟΛΙ
ΦΥΣΑΡΜΟΝΙΚΑ
ΝΤΕΦΙ
ΤΣΕΛΟ
ΚΙΘΑΡΑ
ΤΡΟΜΠΟΝΙ
ΠΙΑΝΟ
ΑΚΟΡΝΤΕΟΝ

REVIEW: EMOTIONS

Review Jumble: The translations in the word list below have been scrambled. Draw lines between the left and right columns to find the correct translations.

X	U	D	O	D	E	S	I	R	P	R	U	S	Δ	Σ	N	A
Σ	T	Σ	Σ	A	U	M	N	E	Y	P	I	K	O	Σ	I	X
O	O	O	O	Ξ	Σ	O	B	O	R	E	D	N	O	Σ	Y	Σ
T	M	N	N	N	A	O	R	A	Y	D	E	Y	Θ	H	O	Y
K	U	A	E	Λ	E	Y	N	P	R	M	E	H	Ά	N	A	Σ
H	D	Φ	M	M	H	M	P	E	Σ	R	M	R	E	E	O	E
Λ	B	H	Ω	S	E	A	Σ	A	M	A	A	M	A	N	E	Σ
Π	Π	P	M	E	H	Δ	I	A	N	Σ	H	S	E	C	O	O
K	Λ	E	Y	Ά	T	Σ	P	T	I	T	I	M	S	N	S	X
E	Y	Π	Θ	D	Y	N	P	E	Σ	Π	Σ	B	E	E	A	Y
M	Π	D	N	O	E	O	E	E	Π	I	O	M	O	N	D	Σ
H	H	B	Θ	D	M	T	I	D	E	M	Y	P	E	Φ	E	H
J	M	N	M	Π	Θ	P	I	Π	I	O	Δ	R	T	A	I	N
K	E	I	A	Ψ	A	A	E	C	P	F	V	S	X	N	R	A
X	N	Λ	R	B	T	Π	A	A	X	O	N	A	N	G	R	Y
Ψ	O	T	I	I	K	E	X	Θ	U	E	M	O	T	I	O	N
Σ	Σ	Y	E	X	E	D	E	S	U	F	N	O	C	H	W	E

EMOTION	ΝΕΥΡΙΚΟΣ
HAPPY	ΠΕΠΕΙΣΜΕΝΟΣ
SAD	ΝΤΡΟΜΠΑΛΟΣ
EXCITED	ΜΠΕΡΔΕΜΕΝΟΣ
BORED	ΕΚΠΛΗΚΤΟΣ
SURPRISED	ΑΙΣΘΗΜΑ
SCARED	ΛΥΠΗΜΕΝΟΣ
ANGRY	ΠΕΡΗΦΑΝΟΣ
CONFUSED	ΘΥΜΩΜΕΝΟΣ
WORRIED	ΑΝΗΣΥΧΟΣ
NERVOUS	ΕΝΘΟΥΣΙΑΣΜΕΝΟΣ
PROUD	ΝΤΡΟΠΙΑΣΜΕΝΟΣ
CONFIDENT	ΦΟΒΙΣΜΕΝΟΣ
EMBARRASSED	ΧΑΡΟΥΜΕΝΟΣ
SHY	ΒΑΡΙΕΣΤΗΜΕΝΟΣ

REVIEW: ILLNESSES

Review Time: Draw lines between the English word on the left and the corresponding translation on the right. Refer back to the original puzzle if you need help.

N	Ώ	N	E	W	D	I	A	R	R	H	E	A	X	E	E
H	Π	I	Ρ	Γ	I	N	F	E	C	T	I	O	N	Ό	Π
T	E	S	P	M	A	R	C	Σ	A	O	P	Д	R	Y	O
Σ	Ξ	Ю	Φ	D	B	R	H	A	J	N	U	O	A	T	N
A	A	N	O	S	E	B	L	E	E	D	D	G	S	L	O
I	N	Ю	A	V	T	L	N	K	A	A	O	T	H	K	K
Γ	Θ	E	E	U	E	M	C	A	Д	D	R	K	I	Λ	E
A	H	F	M	R	S	I	Δ	O	Y	O	A	Λ	I	A	Φ
P	M	Σ	G	O	H	E	M	I	K	T	A	C	Я	Ά	A
P	A	Y	N	C	B	O	A	E	A	Φ	I	E	H	O	Λ
O	E	U	O	Y	Ώ	Λ	H	O	E	P	Γ	A	X	E	O
M	Ξ	L	O	X	Λ	F	O	K	Π	Y	P	E	T	O	Σ
I	D	F	Ω	O	E	O	Γ	Γ	W	H	E	O	I	A	A
A	Ξ	Δ	M	K	A	E	M	C	I	H	Λ	Π	I	A	X
B	N	Я	S	Я	K	P	Y	Ω	M	A	Λ	Ω	Ώ	A	H
K	P	A	M	Π	E	Σ	H	T	H	B	A	I	Δ	D	B

ALLERGY	ΓΡΙΠΗ
CHICKENPOX	ΑΙΜΟΡΡΑΓΙΑ ΣΤΗΝ μυτη
COLD	ΠΥΡΕΤΟΣ
COUGH	ΒΗΧΑΣ
CRAMPS	ΠΟΝΟΚΕΦΑΛΟΣ
DIABETES	ΑΛΛΕΡΓΙΑ
DIARRHEA	ΚΡΑΜΠΕΣ
FEVER	ΑΝΕΜΟΒΛΟΓΙΑ
FLU	ΜΟΛΥΝΣΗ
HEADACHE	ΚΡΥΩΜΑ
INFECTION	ΕΞΑΝΘΗΜΑ
NAUSEA	ΕΓΚΕΦΑΛΙΚΟ
NOSEBLEED	ΔΙΑΡΡΟΙΑ
RASH	ΝΑΥΤΙΑ
STROKE	ΔΙΑΒΗΤΗΣ

REVIEW: ILLNESSES 2

Review Jumble: The translations in the word list below have been scrambled. Draw lines between the left and right columns to find the correct translations.

Η Λ Ο Β Σ Ο Ρ Π Η Κ Α Ι Δ Ρ Α Κ
F Δ Ι Α Σ Ε Ι Σ Η Ι F Ε Β Α Μ Α
Σ Ε Α Η C Η Δ Γ Ν S Π U Μ Ι Ε Τ
Ο Η S U R Ι V Α Ε Ι R Η Ν Ν Ρ Α
Ν Ε Τ Ι Λ Α Ρ Α Λ Ν Χ Ο Η Α Τ Γ
Ο Α Η R Ω Κ Ε Η Η Υ Ι Ό Χ Λ Σ Μ
Π R Μ C Ι Σ Ψ Υ Τ S Ο Α Ν Ε Α Α
Ο Τ Α Μ Α Ι Η Α S Ε Ρ Γ R Μ Ι Α
Χ Α Η Ο Α Η D U Μ Ρ Ο Μ Α G Δ D
Α Τ Ν Ε D Ι C C Α Ε Ε Τ U Μ Ι Я
Μ Τ Ι G Η Ν Ύ Α Κ Ю Α L Τ Μ Ν Μ
Ο Α Α D Ο Υ Α Α Μ Ε Ε S Ι U R Β
Τ C R C Α Α Ψ Σ Ε Ο D Α L Ρ C Γ
Σ Κ Ρ Μ Ω Ι F R Α C Τ U R Ε Ε Τ
Τ Τ S Α Μ Θ Σ Α Ο Ο Ν S R Θ S Ε
Ρ Ε D Ο Μ Ι Ψ Ο Κ Ю Φ Β Ι Π Ζ Я

ACCIDENT	ΚΟΨΙΜΟ
ASTHMA	ΙΛΑΡΑ
BRUISE	ΙΩΣΗ
BURN	ΔΙΑΣΤΡΕΜΑ
CONCUSSION	ΚΑΡΔΙΑΚΗ ΠΡΟΣΒΟΛΗ
CUT	ΑΤΥΧΗΜΑ
EPILEPSY	ΗΜΙΚΡΑΝΙΑ
FRACTURE	ΚΑΨΙΜΟ
HEART ATTACK	ΜΑΓΟΥΛΑΔΕΣ
MEASLES	ΔΙΑΣΕΙΣΗ
MIGRAINE	ΚΑΤΑΓΜΑ
MUMPS	ΕΠΙΛΗΨΙΑ
SPRAIN	ΑΣΘΜΑ
STOMACH ACHE	ΣΤΟΜΑΧΟΠΟΝΟΣ
VIRUS	ΜΕΛΑΝΙΑ

REVIEW: QUESTIONS

Review Time: Draw lines between the English word on the left and the corresponding translation on the right. Refer back to the original puzzle if you need help.

A E W O H O W M U C H Я O U Ω

Ξ M C V Z Δ Γ I A T I P A M N

Λ T B H Ό I Ύ Λ Ί X Ό I E A M

K C O E H U Λ Λ H D P T M Π T

W H A T C O O C O K O E U I E

M T T N Π A T Y A Π B X S O Π

Γ T I A Y X U M E O O I N Ω E

Y I Σ Ω Π O O S H R E Σ Σ T I

O O Ύ A P Σ U Θ E M A E O O Δ

Π R R Ώ O A H H I R I W C Π H

O A I Π E Σ E T E Σ E Y O A R

I F T W E Δ T Ί A L G H H H R

O W E T H A O I N N P W W N Д

Σ O E E H E Σ O E A M M O Q O

G H O W M A N Y E Y I E E N Я

BECAUSE	ΠΩΣ
HOW	ΠΟΤΕ
HOW ARE YOU	ΕΠΕΙΔΗ
HOW FAR	μπορειτε ΝΑ ΜΕ ΒΟΗΘΗΣΕΤΕ
HOW MANY	ΤΙ ΩΡΑ ΕΊΝΑΙ
HOW MUCH	ΠΟΥ
CAN YOU HELP ME	ΠΟΣΟ ΠΟΛΎ
WHAT	ΓΙΑΤΙ
WHAT TIME IS IT	ΠΟΣΟ ΜΑΚΡΙΑ
WHEN	ΠΟΙΟΣ
WHERE	ΠΟΣΑ ΠΟΛΛΑ
WHO	ΠΩΣ ΕΙΣΑΙ
WHY	ΤΙ

REVIEW: AT A RESTAURANT

Review Jumble: The translations in the word list below have been scrambled. Draw lines between the left and right columns to find the correct translations.

P	T	K	Σ	O	N	I	Δ	A	P	B	X	Γ	D	B	E	V
E	H	A	Σ	E	P	B	I	T	O	P	O	Σ	A	Ά	R	R
N	H	T	E	M	T	Ξ	B	Δ	N	L	L	I	B	E	H	T
X	Θ	A	T	Σ	A	E	T	R	T	R	E	S	S	E	D	M
L	Ξ	Λ	E	O	X	Λ	Σ	R	E	Z	I	T	E	P	P	A
A	O	O	Λ	M	M	T	M	T	A	A	R	N	A	H	U	I
B	N	Γ	A	Σ	O	Π	S	H	E	O	K	M	M	Ω	Y	N
R	A	O	Y	A	T	I	Ю	I	O	Π	H	F	T	E	A	C
S	I	Σ	O	I	A	N	Π	M	L	P	O	Ά	A	P	N	O
H	P	M	T	P	I	Ω	S	P	Ω	E	D	T	K	S	E	U
C	E	E	X	A	Π	F	M	Δ	O	K	N	I	P	T	T	R
N	M	K	N	Γ	Σ	P	O	Ά	M	Δ	N	I	N	A	A	S
U	H	P	C	O	Ω	Λ	Ω	E	Ψ	S	I	I	W	N	X	E
L	Σ	A	A	Λ	I	Ω	N	I	I	Я	Ό	Π	R	Θ	E	P
E	E	Σ	F	Φ	P	O	X	V	N	N	V	I	E	D	T	R
Z	M	I	H	T	Y	Y	E	O	O	O	R	E	T	I	A	W
Ω	Ί	A	G	O	K	I	T	K	E	P	O	Ω	P	P	Φ	Φ

APPETIZER	ΜΕΣΗΜΕΡΙΑΝΟ
BREAKFAST	ΧΑΡΤΟΠΕΤΣΕΤΕΣ
DESSERT	ΒΡΑΔΙΝΟ
DINNER	ΦΙΛΟΔΩΡΗΜΑ
DRINK	ΣΕΡΒΙΤΟΡΟΣ
EAT	ΛΟΓΑΡΙΑΣΜΟΣ
LUNCH	ΚΥΡΙΩΣ ΠΙΑΤΟ
MAIN COURSE	ΟΡΕΚΤΙΚΟ
MENU	ΕΠΙΔΟΡΠΙΟ
NAPKINS	ΜΕΝΟΥ
RESTROOMS	ΠΡΩΙΝΟ
THE BILL	ΚΑΤΑΛΟΓΟΣ ΜΕ ΚΡΑΣΙΑ
TIP	ΠΙΝΩ
WAITER	ΤΟΥΑΛΕΤΕΣ
WINE LIST	ΤΡΩΩ

REVIEW: AT THE HOTEL

Review Time: Draw lines between the English word on the left and the corresponding translation on the right. Refer back to the original puzzle if you need help.

Я	Λ	Ό	N	R	I	N	T	E	R	N	E	T	A	S	Π	O
G	B	R	U	T	S	I	D	T	O	N	O	D	I	Я	E	Y
L	E	W	O	T	T	E	L	E	V	I	S	I	O	N	H	O
Δ	L	E	T	O	H	T	Ί	U	L	K	Λ	E	I	Δ	I	I
Ω	A	Ό	A	H	M	A	E	E	G	T	F	C	T	P	E	T
M	E	L	Я	O	Γ	S	T	L	Д	G	Ю	B	H	M	Ω	A
A	T	N	O	I	T	P	E	C	E	R	A	T	Y	B	T	M
T	I	Σ	Я	O	A	K	N	R	T	P	Σ	G	D	L	K	Ω
I	E	Y	E	P	I	O	B	H	V	A	H	O	E	A	O	Δ
O	Λ	N	E	Y	R	E	Λ	Γ	N	I	N	O	B	N	Y	A
H	X	R	P	K	E	E	X	M	T	Ω	C	Π	N	K	B	I
X	O	O	H	E	O	K	Y	O	Φ	T	E	E	F	E	E	Σ
O	N	O	E	P	T	Γ	Σ	E	Δ	T	A	Σ	M	T	P	E
Δ	E	M	A	T	H	N	Λ	O	Σ	O	E	B	T	S	T	P
O	N	Σ	T	Q	O	H	I	E	Π	A	N	T	O	Ί	E	H
Π	H	X	A	P	T	I	T	O	Y	A	Λ	E	T	A	Σ	Π
Y	M	K	P	E	B	A	T	I	Ό	L	Ώ	K	Ξ	I	S	Y

BED
BLANKETS
DO NOT DISTURB
GYM
HOTEL
INTERNET
KEY
LUGGAGE
RECEPTION
ROOM
ROOM SERVICE
TELEPHONE
TELEVISION
TOILET PAPER
TOWEL

INTEPNET
ΥΠΟΔΟΧΗ
ΠΕΤΣΕΤΑ
ΔΩΜΑΤΙΟ
ΚΟΥΒΕΡΤΕΣ
ΑΠΟΣΚΕΥΕΣ
ΤΗΛΕΟΡΑΣΗ
ΓΥΜΝΑΣΤΗΡΙΟ
ΞΕΝΟΔΟΧΕΙΟ
ΧΑΡΤΙ ΤΟΥΑΛΕΤΑΣ
ΚΛΕΙΔΙ
ΚΡΕΒΑΤΙ
ΥΠΗΡΕΣΙΑ ΔΩΜΑΤΙΟΥ
ΜΗΝ ΕΝΟΧΛΕΙΤΕ
ΤΗΛΕΦΩΝΟ

REVIEW: SUBJECTS

Review Jumble: The translations in the word list below have been scrambled. Draw lines between the left and right columns to find the correct translations.

B	I	H	T	A	M	U	S	I	C	Y	T	N	S	A	Ί	Σ
I	E	Σ	H	Y	G	E	O	G	R	A	P	H	Y	P	E	N
O	E	Ψ	T	Γ	R	E	D	O	Ώ	H	R	G	Ά	Π	Ί	N
Λ	Σ	A	Φ	O	E	T	T	I	I	Д	O	T	I	Д	N	S
O	E	Я	K	Φ	P	S	S	L	C	L	E	X	S	M	S	E
Γ	A	N	R	I	I	I	O	I	O	I	E	K	S	E	C	G
I	E	P	G	H	T	S	A	I	M	I	N	A	E	O	I	A
A	H	I	K	I	O	A	B	E	P	E	K	E	N	H	E	U
I	K	R	A	P	N	Φ	M	H	Π	I	H	O	I	K	N	G
Φ	I	I	H	I	Y	E	Σ	H	M	I	M	C	S	I	C	N
O	N	Y	T	Σ	Φ	E	E	O	Θ	I	Σ	C	U	Σ	E	A
Σ	A	N	I	Σ	I	A	N	R	C	A	I	T	B	Y	Z	L
O	X	K	C	Σ	A	O	P	S	I	S	M	Θ	H	O	Ύ	S
Λ	H	M	H	Ω	K	K	A	Γ	Y	N	A	I	E	M	H	X
I	M	P	I	I	Ω	O	I	H	Ω	E	G	O	V	Z	E	Σ
Φ	B	I	O	B	N	Θ	P	E	Σ	E	Σ	Σ	Ω	Λ	Γ	Σ
B	P	A	U	H	K	I	P	T	A	I	Γ	Σ	A	A	Ί	B

ART	ΙΑΤΡΙΚΗ
BIOLOGY	ΜΗΧΑΝΙΚΗ
BUSINESS	ΜΟΥΣΙΚΗ
CHEMISTRY	ΓΕΩΓΡΑΦΙΑ
ECONOMICS	ΓΛΩΣΣΕΣ
ENGINEERING	ΕΠΙΧΕΙΡΗΣΕΙΣ
GEOGRAPHY	ΜΑΘΗΜΑΤΙΚΑ
HISTORY	ΦΥΣΙΚΗ
LANGUAGES	ΟΙΚΟΝΟΜΙΚΑ
MATH	ΧΗΜΕΙΑ
MEDICINE	ΕΙΚΑΣΤΙΚΑ
MUSIC	ΦΙΛΟΣΟΦΙΑ
PHILOSOPHY	ΕΠΙΣΤΗΜΕΣ
PHYSICS	ΙΣΤΟΡΙΑ
SCIENCE	ΒΙΟΛΟΓΙΑ

REVIEW: MATH

Review Time: Draw lines between the English word on the left and the corresponding translation on the right. Refer back to the original puzzle if you need help.

```
Y Ά X M F C Δ A Φ A I P E Σ H Σ Π
I R O T U D I V I S I O N L E O A
H K T Ξ Ψ L Σ T V O L U M E Λ K P
Σ Λ A E G A T N E C R E P Λ Ω Γ A
Ω A P P M Z T I Я M P E A Ξ P O Λ
Σ Σ I Π E O E T P B H Π L E Δ S Λ
I M Θ P L T E Δ N L Λ T R U N A H
Ξ A M O T L Y G I A I P I O R D Λ
E T H Σ H E U O Σ A E C I R P D A
N E T Θ O K M I I N I T A A A I F
O Q I E K T A Ω D Π C P R T T T E
I U K Σ L Σ E I E A M A E Ω I I T
T A H H M A C Θ R Γ L O Φ Σ O O H
C T A O T U E T A L T L K I H N N
A I Σ O L O B R E K N O Δ A B M E
R O T A L U C L A C Σ A K A P A X
F N R N S K Ί E O T Σ O Σ O Π R E
```

ADDITION	ΠΑΡΑΛΛΗΛΑ
AREA	ΓΕΩΜΕΤΡΙΑ
ARITHMETIC	ΠΟΛΛΑΠΛΑΣΙΑΣΜΟΣ
CALCULATOR	ΚΑΘΕΤΟΣ
DIVISION	ΠΟΣΟΣΤΟ
EQUATION	ΑΡΙΘΜΗΤΙΚΗ
FRACTION	ΑΦΑΙΡΕΣΗ
GEOMETRY	ΠΡΟΣΘΕΣΗ
MULTIPLICATION	ΔΙΑΙΡΕΣΗ
PARALLEL	ΟΓΚΟΣ
PERCENTAGE	ΧΑΡΑΚΑΣ
PERPENDICULAR	ΚΛΑΣΜΑ
RULER	ΕΜΒΑΔΟΝ
SUBTRACTION	ΚΟΜΠΙΟΥΤΕΡΑΚΙ
VOLUME	ΕΞΙΣΩΣΗ

REVIEW: AT THE AIRPORT

Review Jumble: The translations in the word list below have been scrambled. Draw lines between the left and right columns to find the correct translations.

Σ Ε Σ Τ Ι Λ Α Β Ο Τ J D B G Ε Ύ X
Ο Ι Ρ Η Τ Ι Σ Ι Ε R U N W A Y T E
Μ Η Ε Φ Λ Α Ο Λ Τ Ι C K E T X Ψ S
Θ Η Φ Ξ Τ Υ Ω Υ Τ Ι R U C E S E Σ
Α Δ Σ Η Ι Ν Π Γ Γ Ρ Ε C T E G O O
Τ Σ Χ Ω Ε Φ S L A V I R R A Φ I M
Σ Η Φ Ι Ι Μ Α S F T Θ U G A P M O
Σ Ν Ο Α S Ε S Ώ S H T G K H Ω O P
Ο Θ C Α Λ Ρ Γ Ε Ν R A Σ T F T P Δ
K E U I O E M O A B O A F F E Δ A
I I S R Ύ O I P Π P B Ω A O Γ O I
T Δ T P D D E A E A A R E E X P Δ
A T O O C D B A I N C E E K Ω E O
M H M R M A I Δ Ό R M O M A P A P
P Ώ S T Ά L A N I M R E T T I I E
E L A N O I T A N R E T N I O T A
T B Λ Ω A N A X Ω P H Σ E I Σ T M

AIRCRAFT	ΑΝΑΧΩΡΗΣΕΙΣ
AIRPORT	ΤΕΡΜΑΤΙΚΟΣ ΣΤΑΘΜΟΣ
ARRIVALS	ΕΓΧΩΡΙΟΣ
BAGGAGE	ΤΕΛΩΝΕΙΟ
CUSTOMS	ΑΦΙΞΕΙΣ
DEPARTURES	ΠΥΛΗ
DOMESTIC	ΔΙΕΘΝΗΣ
GATE	ΑΕΡΟΣΚΑΦΟΣ
INTERNATIONAL	ΒΑΛΙΤΣΕΣ
PASSPORT	ΑΣΦΑΛΕΙΑ
RUNWAY	ΔΙΑΒΑΤΗΡΙΟ
SECURITY	ΑΕΡΟΔΡΟΜΙΟ
TAKEOFF	ΑΠΟΓΕΙΩΣΗ
TERMINAL	ΕΙΣΙΤΗΡΙΟ
TICKET	ΑΕΡΟΔΙΑΔΡΟΜΟΣ

REVIEW: ON THE FARM

Review Time: Draw lines between the English word on the left and the corresponding translation on the right. Refer back to the original puzzle if you need help.

Σ	S	C	Y	A	Λ	Y	O	Π	O	Λ	A	Γ	Z	L
O	H	R	H	T	W	E	O	B	D	Д	Δ	Π	X	T
P	E	O	C	I	O	I	Ώ	O	A	B	A	I	A	B
A	E	P	R	Σ	C	Ώ	N	C	O	Π	Λ	P	Ώ	U
Δ	P	S	I	S	O	K	K	R	I	X	E	Ю	A	L
I	N	P	A	G	E	P	E	A	O	T	Γ	S	K	L
A	N	A	M	Y	A	T	Y	N	K	B	A	N	O	A
Γ	Ю	Y	H	J	S	Σ	O	A	Ό	M	Δ	Д	T	M
I	H	R	O	O	A	Γ	P	O	T	H	Σ	E	O	B
Δ	T	A	O	P	A	T	P	A	Π	Σ	E	C	Π	N
A	Ό	R	O	T	Y	K	Π	P	O	B	A	T	O	I
Ό	X	K	A	E	C	O	H	Σ	T	Ю	N	Y	Y	H
L	O	O	O	U	A	A	Γ	B	E	O	Γ	O	Λ	A
K	G	H	D	Ξ	F	A	R	M	E	R	Ψ	E	O	W
O	I	Ξ	Y	E	K	R	U	T	I	Y	Φ	F	S	U

BULL	ΑΛΟΓΟ
CHICKEN	ΓΑΙΔΑΡΟΣ
COW	ΓΑΛΟΠΟΥΛΑ
CROPS	ΑΡΝΙ
DONKEY	ΑΓΕΛΑΔΑ
DUCK	ΤΑΥΡΟΣ
FARMER	ΠΑΠΙΑ
GOAT	ΓΟΥΡΟΥΝΙ
HORSE	ΚΟΤΟΠΟΥΛΟ
LAMB	ΣΠΑΡΤΑ
PIG	ΤΡΑΚΤΕΡ
ROOSTER	ΚΟΚΟΡΑΣ
SHEEP	ΑΓΡΟΤΗΣ
TRACTOR	ΠΡΟΒΑΤΟ
TURKEY	ΓΙΔΑ

REVIEW: SIGHTSEEING

Review Jumble: The translations in the word list below have been scrambled. Draw lines between the left and right columns to find the correct translations.

X R M Ю X E Σ H T P A X R X G R H
O U Σ U A S N O I T C E R I D N B
N I P Σ S Σ O Γ A N E Ξ N A A E T
Д N A K Σ E Σ Ό S C H F B X I G Λ
M S R T S H U E A R O M H M E U Q
A A T Γ T Θ N M Ί R I M E Σ M I K
P E G N Θ R C X M Γ H N O A H D T
Y D A H E O A A E K H K E A N E O
Я I L R R M T C I T I Δ I V M B U
I U L D E I U Φ T T H Π O P U O R
Ύ G E I O M A N Ω I I Σ Ώ K Д O I
P R R N D P A I O E O I E M P K S
M U Y Λ Γ Ю Δ C P M A N Θ Θ E A T
Y O Θ O P I N E B Y O Σ S I K H Π
K T T D Ξ P Π Λ H P O Φ O P I E Σ
Y Ω Σ A T Σ I P Y O T A P E M A K
Φ A T A E Θ O I Ξ A O I E Σ Y O M

ART GALLERY	ΣΟΥΒΕΝΙΡ
ATTRACTIONS	ΧΑΡΤΗΣ
CAMCORDER	ΕΚΘΕΣΗ ΤΕΧΝΗΣ
CAMERA	ΟΔΗΓΊΕΣ
DIRECTIONS	ΦΩΤΟΓΡΑΦΙΚΗ ΜΗΧΑΝΗ
GUIDE BOOK	ΠΑΡΚΟ
INFORMATION	ΞΕΝΑΓΟΣ
MAP	ΑΞΙΟΘΕΑΤΑ
MONUMENTS	ΜΟΥΣΕΙΟ
MUSEUM	ΜΝΗΜΕΙΑ
PARK	ΤΟΥΡΙΣΤΑΣ
RUINS	ΕΡΕΙΠΙΑ
SOUVENIRS	ΚΑΜΕΡΑ
TOUR GUIDE	ΤΑΞΙΔΙΩΤΙΚΟΣ οδηγοσ
TOURIST	ΠΛΗΡΟΦΟΡΙΕΣ

REVIEW: AT THE BEACH

Review Time: Draw lines between the English word on the left and the corresponding translation on the right. Refer back to the original puzzle if you need help.

Д	E	M	W	A	V	E	S	M	N	G	Φ	K	F	X	Δ
A	M	M	O	Σ	H	T	Σ	Ω	Σ	O	Γ	A	Y	A	N
G	O	S	W	I	M	M	I	N	G	N	O	Π	Ξ	I	Ω
H	M	E	O	K	Θ	O	D	M	K	Σ	Θ	E	O	U	Y
Σ	M	S	L	E	Ω	K	E	A	N	O	Σ	Λ	B	Д	O
E	A	S	E	T	H	Ω	T	Λ	K	I	Λ	O	C	E	I
P	Ό	A	U	A	S	A	T	A	Δ	Λ	G	Y	H	O	Λ
Φ	Π	L	Δ	N	M	A	I	X	D	H	N	A	M	Ί	H
T	A	G	I	Y	S	Λ	C	Θ	Q	Π	I	U	Ξ	Π	A
Y	O	N	K	F	H	C	A	D	A	E	F	T	S	A	I
A	P	U	N	I	E	Λ	R	P	N	B	R	Ψ	A	S	Λ
P	T	S	T	K	A	G	A	E	U	A	U	A	O	H	A
A	Σ	N	Ώ	Σ	N	Λ	U	M	E	T	S	C	P	O	Y
K	A	I	Σ	K	I	D	N	A	S	N	E	B	K	V	Γ
I	K	A	Δ	A	B	Y	O	K	R	A	H	C	A	E	B
D	Λ	G	K	A	B	F	Ά	U	N	D	H	X	I	L	T

BEACH
BUCKET
HAT
LIFE GUARD
OCEAN
SAND
SANDCASTLE
SEA
SHOVEL
SUN
SUNGLASSES
SUNSCREEN
SURFING
SWIMMING
WAVES

ΩΚΕΑΝΟΣ
ΦΤΥΑΡΑΚΙ
ΝΑΥΑΓΟΣΩΣΤΗΣ
ΑΜΜΟΣ
ΚΑΠΕΛΟ
ΠΑΡΑΛΙΑ
ΑΝΤΙΗΛΙΑΚΟ
ΘΑΛΑΣΣΑ
ΚΥΜΑΤΑ
ΗΛΙΟΣ
ΚΑΣΤΡΟ ΑΠΌ ΑΜΜΟ
ΚΟΛΥΜΠΙ
ΓΥΑΛΙΑ ΗΛΙΟΥ
ΚΟΥΒΑΔΑΚΙ
ΣΕΡΦ

REVIEW: OPPOSITES 1

Review Jumble: The translations in the word list below have been scrambled. Draw lines between the left and right columns to find the correct translations.

Ψ E H K Π X N Σ Ώ Ю F L Ί Ύ B
L L A T I H O T O H E Я S T T
N L R Σ L N F Ά X Λ P E H X R
Ό A D L E O Ю Σ O Λ H Ψ A A E
E M R T S E W E T Ά Y Ψ H M N
Σ S Σ R H D A B T H Д I Y H Ю
Ю O O L O I R Σ Π B Ί T M Λ B
X R K Ό R W O Y Λ H T B Y O F
B T A A T P C Σ A O I Γ L Σ R
O Δ Λ Ό K Ξ O X T G P G O O I
Ύ Y A I T N E P Y O O T H Λ N
Θ P M E Γ A Λ O Σ O N P D A H
D O Δ E R Ύ E A D O T Ά M K Φ
Z Γ T Γ Ψ Ξ A K K K Ψ I N Ю Δ
G Σ O P H Λ K Σ Ω Ύ T M O Ξ T

BIG	ΜΙΚΡΟΣ
SMALL	ΨΗΛΟΣ
WIDE	ΣΚΛΗΡΟΣ
NARROW	ΧΑΜΗΛΟΣ
TALL	ΣΤΕΝΟΣ
SHORT	ΣΤΕΓΝΟΣ
HIGH	ΚΑΚΟΣ
LOW	ΥΓΡΟΣ
GOOD	ΚΑΛΟΣ
BAD	ΥΨΗΛΟΣ
WET	ΜΕΓΑΛΟΣ
DRY	ΜΑΛΑΚΟΣ
HARD	ΚΟΝΤΟΣ
SOFT	ΠΛΑΤΥΣ

REVIEW: OPPOSITES 2

Review Time: Draw lines between the English word on the left and the corresponding translation on the right. Refer back to the original puzzle if you need help.

D Ώ Θ H F T V D S A A T Y J Σ
H K T H T Ύ I E F Ύ T P I T Λ
F D L O C R O Σ O Γ P A O A Ω
O G Я L T P T Ά O Ю T E Θ O Ά
F Ξ E Y E Ψ N K T T A O T Ю Ψ
G A M N I Ώ P H A N Σ I Z Σ Θ
N E S Ψ U Σ E Γ Σ Θ A Ω E K O
O V D T Q O A B P Y A H Σ Λ P
R I G H T Y L N E H X P T E Y
W S K A K P I B O Σ Γ O O I B
N N W N H K F M H I H O Σ Σ Ω
D E S O L C H E A P X O P T Δ
L P T I L T E E L P E T N O H
V X I S H S B P Ω M I K O Σ Σ
H E N Y Γ U N A Φ T H N O Σ H

FAST	ΓΡΗΓΟΡΟΣ
SLOW	ΑΡΓΟΣ
RIGHT	ΚΛΕΙΣΤΟΣ
WRONG	ΦΤΗΝΟΣ
CLEAN	ΖΕΣΤΟΣ
DIRTY	ΒΡΩΜΙΚΟΣ
QUIET	ΚΑΘΑΡΟΣ
NOISY	ΗΣΥΧΟΣ
EXPENSIVE	ΚΡΥΟΣ
CHEAP	ΑΚΡΙΒΟΣ
HOT	ΘΟΡΥΒΩΔΗΣ
COLD	ΛΑΘΟΣ
OPEN	ΣΩΣΤΟΣ
CLOSED	ΑΝΟΙΧΤΟΣ

REVIEW: OPPOSITES 3

Review Jumble: The translations in the word list below have been scrambled. Draw lines between the left and right columns to find the correct translations.

L	Ί	C	O	A	Π	J	A	Π	K	Y	S	H	D	A
I	Σ	K	Σ	O	I	E	Δ	A	D	T	T	A	F	Y
G	Ω	K	Σ	O	N	O	A	Λ	E	L	R	P	M	S
H	P	B	O	I	T	E	Σ	I	E	K	O	G	M	A
T	S	F	Λ	T	Ю	A	O	O	Θ	A	N	E	W	E
Я	L	O	E	X	E	Z	N	Σ	M	I	G	Ю	Σ	W
Φ	T	U	T	I	N	I	O	Y	N	A	Y	A	Δ	A
Ю	S	A	C	Z	L	N	N	N	Δ	Σ	N	Y	H	Σ
Ю	B	Θ	I	I	I	N	I	O	O	H	Σ	Y	O	O
Π	D	K	Λ	E	F	G	D	Λ	Σ	K	O	P	Δ	T
H	N	H	T	R	E	F	O	N	O	C	T	M	Γ	A
Y	R	Ω	Γ	B	U	K	I	Λ	E	N	Π	S	Γ	M
Y	Φ	M	E	L	Y	H	O	D	O	T	E	F	Σ	E
Ω	H	A	L	E	T	Σ	H	X	P	A	Λ	Ю	T	Γ
C	Ό	T	Ό	O	O	S	T	Ξ	K	A	E	W	O	M

FULL	ΔΥΣΚΟΛΟΣ
EMPTY	ΔΥΝΑΤΟΣ
NEW	ΑΔΥΝΑΜΟΣ
OLD	ΑΡΧΗ
LIGHT	ΦΩΤΕΙΝΟΣ
DARK	ΛΕΠΤΟΣ
EASY	ΕΥΚΟΛΟΣ
DIFFICULT	ΠΑΛΙΟΣ
STRONG	ΝΕΟΣ
WEAK	ΑΔΕΙΟΣ
FAT	ΓΕΜΑΤΟΣ
THIN	ΤΕΛΟΣ
BEGINNING	ΧΟΝΤΡΟΣ
END	ΣΚΟΤΕΙΝΟΣ

REVIEW: OPPOSITES 4

Review Time: Draw lines between the English word on the left and the corresponding translation on the right. Refer back to the original puzzle if you need help.

U	I	F	E	I	W	E	A	Ψ	O	A	A	E	I	O
A	N	X	D	V	M	U	T	I	B	Ά	D	F	Φ	I
Π	N	C	I	L	Ю	Ψ	Д	M	E	O	Ξ	X	D	O
P	T	A	S	I	Ό	E	I	A	F	L	E	Y	R	Ά
Ω	A	N	N	Σ	F	A	R	S	O	D	A	Д	H	T
T	Σ	O	I	E	I	L	E	J	R	Π	A	T	K	V
O	E	Δ	Ώ	Ώ	Y	R	E	R	E	H	S	Γ	E	H
Σ	M	Λ	R	M	Θ	A	A	D	X	R	S	O	Σ	Ξ
I	A	Λ	E	E	R	E	H	T	I	W	Ά	M	W	F
P	E	T	M	Y	T	N	A	F	U	S	O	Ω	Ύ	A
Ω	A	K	N	Σ	T	F	A	R	Σ	O	T	S	A	L
X	Γ	I	E	O	I	A	A	B	V	Σ	H	U	N	E
Q	P	T	M	A	K	P	I	A	W	H	B	T	O	O
Π	A	I	A	B	E	Ξ	Ω	O	T	Σ	E	Π	I	O
S	Ί	Λ	Q	Φ	T	S	I	N	Σ	R	E	M	P	W

NEAR	ΠΡΩΤΟΣ
FAR	ΝΩΡΙΣ
HERE	ΕΚΕΙ
THERE	ΜΑΚΡΙΑ
WITH	ΧΩΡΙΣ
WITHOUT	ΜΕ
BEFORE	ΜΕΣΑ
AFTER	ΤΕΛΕΥΤΑΙΟΣ
EARLY	ΕΔΏ
LATE	ΜΕΤΑ
INSIDE	ΚΟΝΤΑ
OUTSIDE	ΕΞΩ
FIRST	ΠΡΙΝ
LAST	ΑΡΓΑ

REVIEW: MATERIALS

Review Jumble: The translations in the word list below have been scrambled. Draw lines between the left and right columns to find the correct translations.

T O C W L O I E I Z Σ O I A Σ
M D N O M A I D Ξ Ί O H I O N
E Ξ O O P E I M K Y K A M S Λ
Σ N Z D O P T R X B Λ M H E E
O Φ O H Θ I E A E H A O Σ E Y
Σ X Ю T Φ S M R L T X S A M K
Y E V M S I P M Ό Y A L C M O
P X T A P L A T I N U M E Д X
X G L P A V O Z D A P T E П P
R G S S T E Δ I A M A N T I Y
Ω I T E B R Λ T Ό Λ Γ Y Ψ O Σ
N I E O G A Σ П Λ A Σ T I K O
C E E O Y A N O T E П M T I Σ
N E L Γ Λ E T E R C N O C Λ O
R D A I G P X N T R E M W Y O

CLAY	ΑΤΣΑΛΙ
CONCRETE	ΓΥΨΟΣ
COPPER	ΞΥΛΟ
DIAMOND	ΜΠΕΤΟΝ
GLASS	ΧΡΥΣΟΣ
GOLD	ΜΕΤΑΛΛΟ
MATERIAL	ΑΜΜΟΣ
METAL	ΑΣΗΜΙ
PLASTIC	ΠΕΤΡΑ
PLATINUM	ΔΙΑΜΑΝΤΙ
SAND	ΛΕΥΚΟΧΡΥΣΟΣ
SILVER	ΓΥΑΛΙ
STEEL	ΧΑΛΚΟΣ
STONE	ΥΛΙΚΟ
WOOD	ΠΛΑΣΤΙΚΟ

REVIEW: MATERIALS 2

Review Time: Draw lines between the English word on the left and the corresponding translation on the right. Refer back to the original puzzle if you need help.

I	C	M	G	O	R	T	A	Ю	L	Γ	B	O	O	S	F
Λ	O	Q	N	Σ	Σ	N	Y	Λ	C	I	Д	T	I	T	H
A	Ξ	B	I	I	Λ	A	N	A	H	I	O	S	O	A	T
Σ	I	S	M	Δ	O	A	M	P	E	Δ	M	S	M	I	N
T	S	E	O	E	P	Ω	Σ	R	O	R	T	A	A	N	E
A	N	B	P	P	X	T	E	T	E	Z	P	R	R	L	M
O	M	A	A	O	T	W	K	H	I	B	O	B	B	E	E
T	N	M	M	Ю	A	E	T	O	R	X	B	Σ	L	S	C
Ω	A	B	P	A	P	A	C	I	A	E	O	U	E	S	O
Δ	Ψ	A	A	A	E	J	C	P	T	Z	P	C	R	S	T
I	A	K	M	L	L	K	T	N	T	A	D	A	X	T	T
E	O	I	N	A	T	I	T	Y	O	Д	N	A	P	E	O
Ξ	K	H	O	P	E	I	O	B	Ψ	R	H	I	E	E	N
O	Λ	B	Y	O	T	P	Ύ	M	U	N	I	M	U	L	A
N	Ύ	B	A	B	Π	S	Σ	O	Δ	B	Y	Λ	O	M	O
A	Λ	O	Y	M	I	N	I	O	Ό	E	R	O	M	T	A

ALUMINUM	ΤΟΥΒΛΟ
BRASS	ΧΩΜΑ
BRICK	ΒΑΜΒΑΚΙ
CEMENT	ΔΕΡΜΑ
CERAMIC	ΑΛΟΥΜΙΝΙΟ
COTTON	ΛΑΣΤΙΧΟ
IRON	ΧΑΡΤΙ
LEAD	ΚΕΡΑΜΙΚΟ
LEATHER	ΑΝΟΞΕΙΔΩΤΟ ΑΤΣΑΛΙ
MARBLE	ΜΟΛΥΒΔΟΣ
PAPER	ΤΣΙΜΕΝΟ
RUBBER	ΜΑΡΜΑΡΟ
SOIL	ΣΙΔΕΡΟ
STAINLESS STEEL	ΜΠΡΟΥΤΖΟΣ
TITANIUM	ΤΙΤΑΝΙΟ

REVIEW: SOMETHING TO DRINK?

Review Jumble: The translations in the word list below have been scrambled. Draw lines between the left and right columns to find the correct translations.

Y	O	I	H	K	W	Ί	N	Δ	E	G	N	G	I	U
D	A	N	I	K	A	Φ	E	Σ	H	Д	Σ	Σ	Ύ	G
N	I	G	Σ	Ώ	R	Π	I	I	N	O	A	Ί	A	B
A	H	Π	A	N	E	P	O	M	M	P	M	A	N	Z
R	M	Π	P	A	N	T	I	Y	K	Ψ	Π	Λ	Λ	T
B	U	O	K	K	O	R	X	O	T	R	A	Ί	Σ	O
P	W	M	O	T	Y	N	K	P	E	Σ	N	A	A	E
T	H	K	N	O	N	Y	I	E	G	K	I	Λ	A	Я
W	I	I	I	B	E	I	B	C	L	O	A	N	T	R
H	T	O	K	Λ	S	A	E	I	C	Γ	Д	T	O	E
I	E	W	K	Σ	D	A	M	U	Ί	U	H	Ю	E	T
S	W	Ύ	O	N	I	Z	T	J	T	C	P	F	K	A
K	I	Λ	K	A	P	Y	Π	M	N	O	F	P	O	W
E	N	I	W	D	E	R	O	I	V	O	D	K	A	Π
Y	E	N	G	A	P	M	A	H	C	O	R	B	M	C

BEER	ΚΟΚΚΙΝΟ ΚΡΑΣΙ
BRANDY	ΛΕΥΚΟ ΚΡΑΣΙ
CAPPUCCINO	ΚΑΦΕΣ
CHAMPAGNE	ΧΥΜΟΣ
COFFEE	ΒΟΤΚΑ
GIN	ΜΠΥΡΑ
JUICE	ΟΥΙΣΚΙ
MILK	ΝΕΡΟ
RED WINE	ΓΑΛΑ
RUM	ΚΑΠΟΥΤΣΙΝΟ
TEA	ΤΣΑΙ
VODKA	ΡΟΥΜΙ
WATER	ΜΠΡΑΝΤΙ
WHISKEY	ΣΑΜΠΑΝΙΑ
WHITE WINE	ΤΖΙΝ

SOLUTIONS

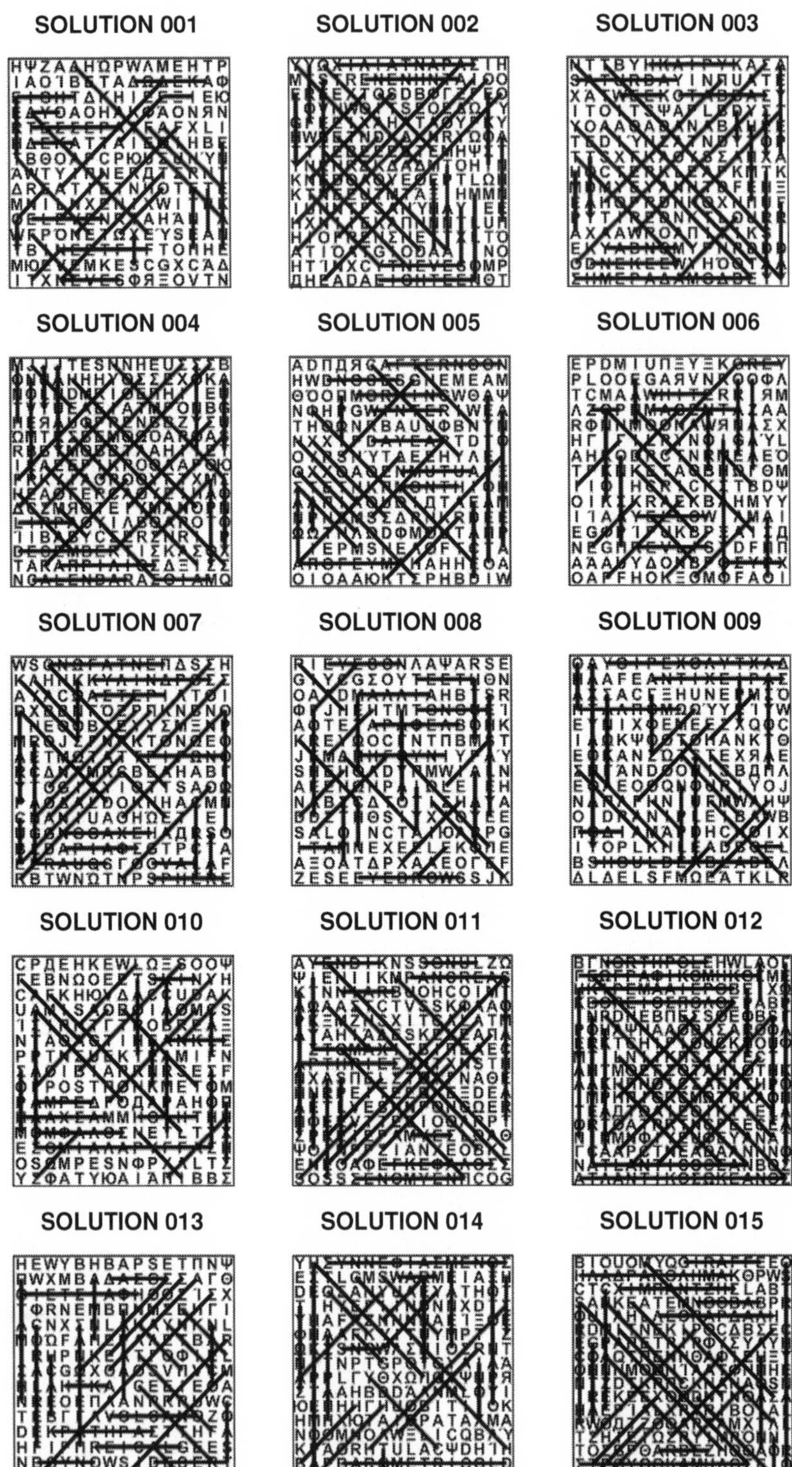
SOLUTION 001
SOLUTION 002
SOLUTION 003
SOLUTION 004
SOLUTION 005
SOLUTION 006
SOLUTION 007
SOLUTION 008
SOLUTION 009
SOLUTION 010
SOLUTION 011
SOLUTION 012
SOLUTION 013
SOLUTION 014
SOLUTION 015

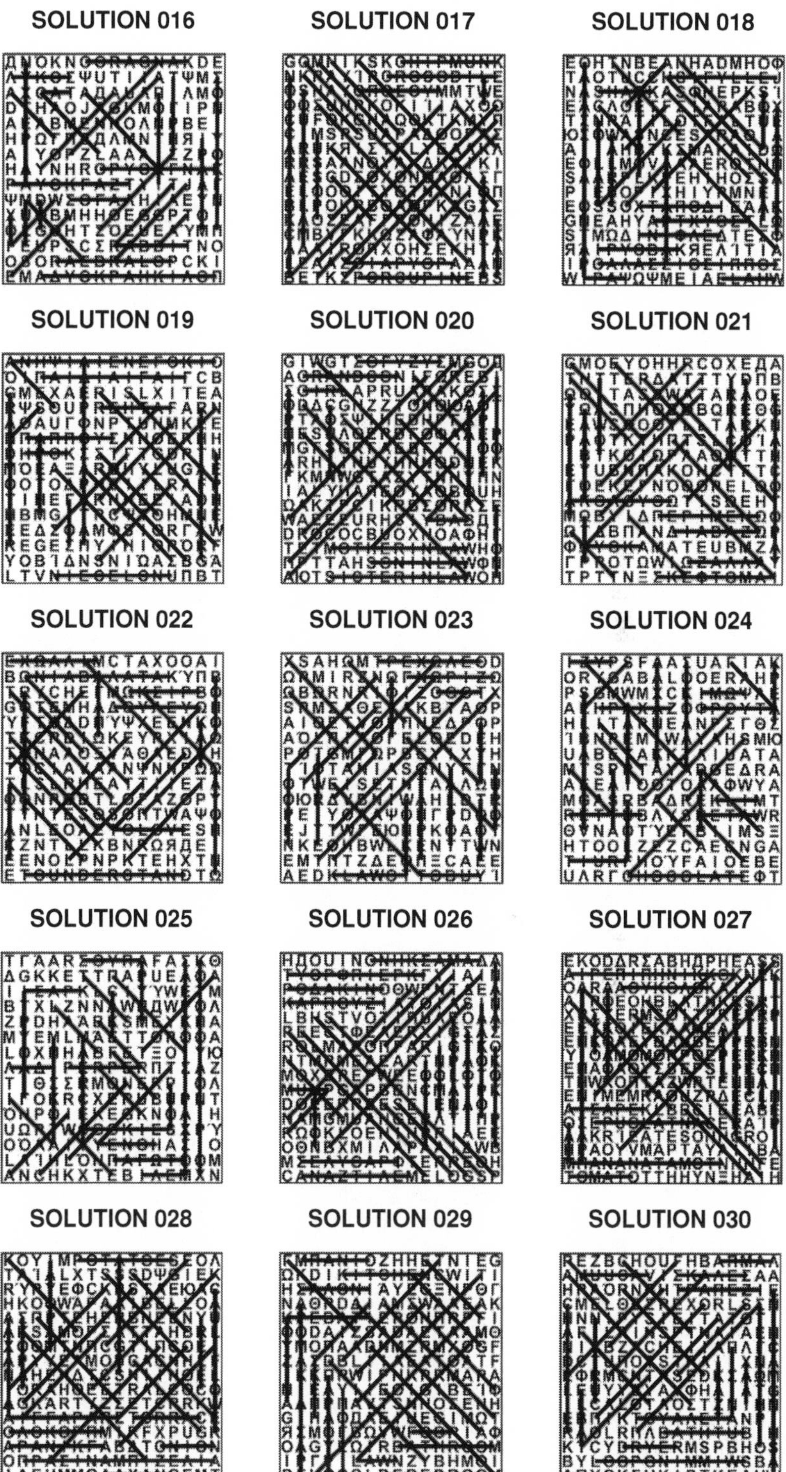

SOLUTION 016 SOLUTION 017 SOLUTION 018 SOLUTION 019 SOLUTION 020 SOLUTION 021 SOLUTION 022 SOLUTION 023 SOLUTION 024 SOLUTION 025 SOLUTION 026 SOLUTION 027 SOLUTION 028 SOLUTION 029 SOLUTION 030

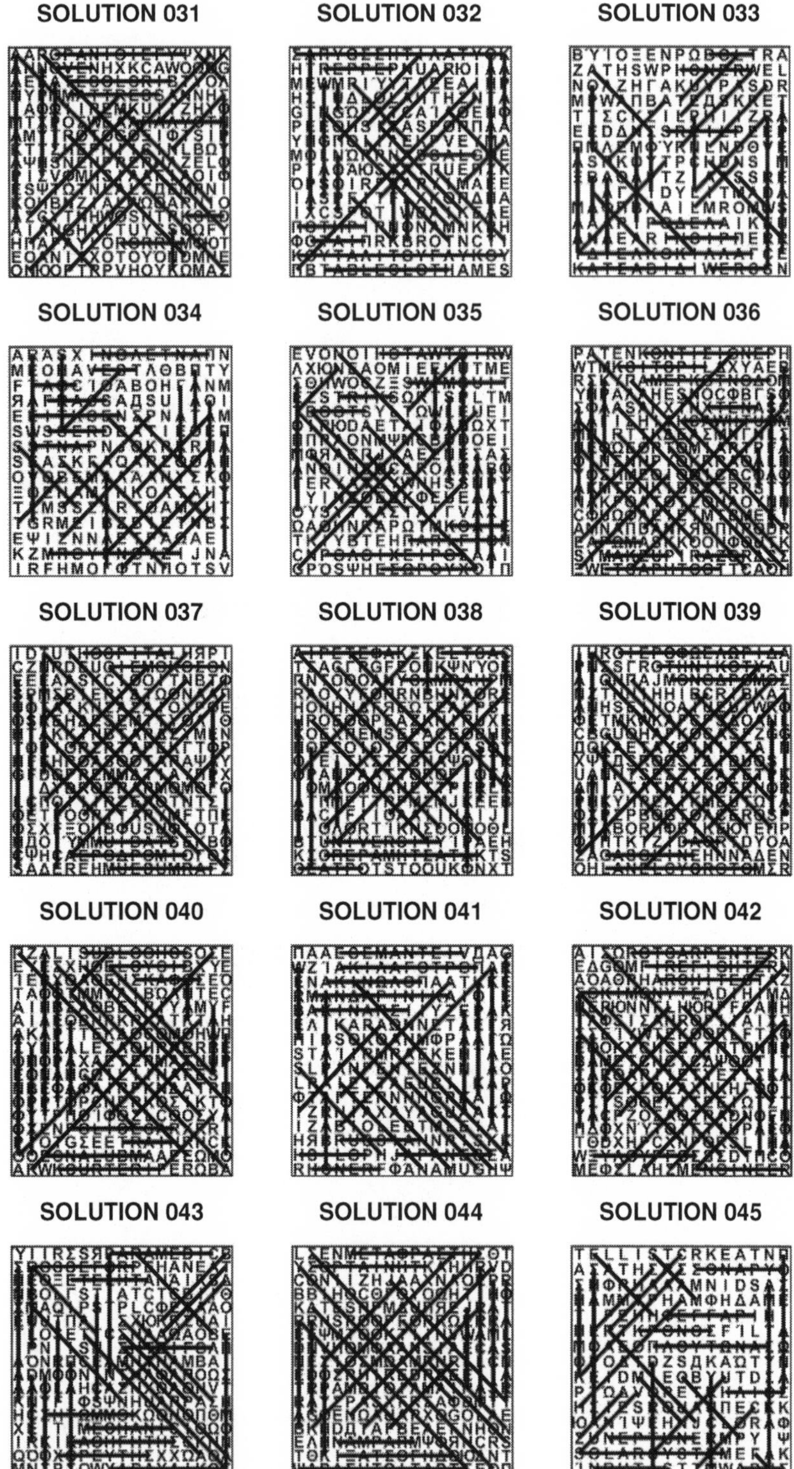
SOLUTION 031
SOLUTION 032
SOLUTION 033
SOLUTION 034
SOLUTION 035
SOLUTION 036
SOLUTION 037
SOLUTION 038
SOLUTION 039
SOLUTION 040
SOLUTION 041
SOLUTION 042
SOLUTION 043
SOLUTION 044
SOLUTION 045

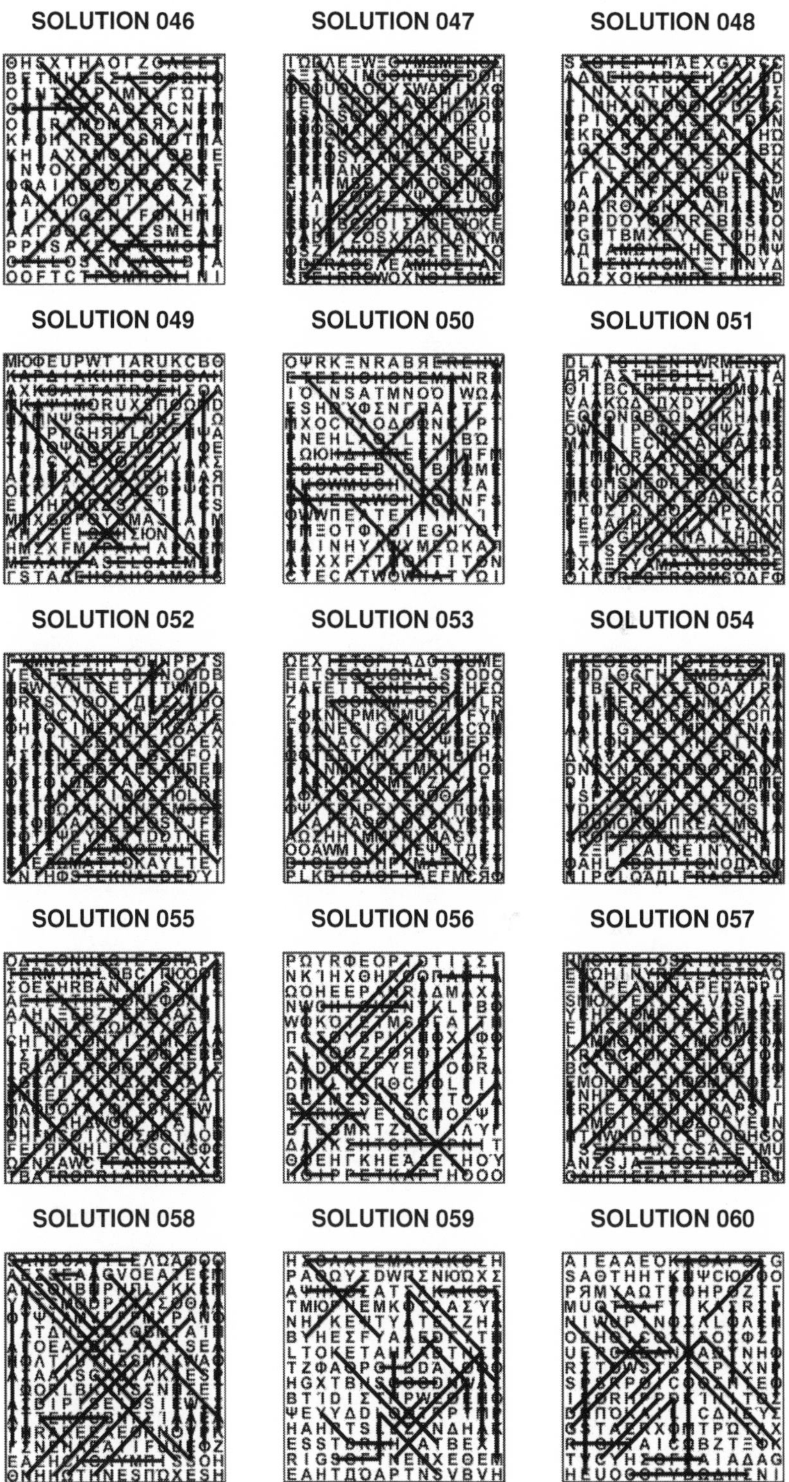

SOLUTION 046
SOLUTION 047
SOLUTION 048
SOLUTION 049
SOLUTION 050
SOLUTION 051
SOLUTION 052
SOLUTION 053
SOLUTION 054
SOLUTION 055
SOLUTION 056
SOLUTION 057
SOLUTION 058
SOLUTION 059
SOLUTION 060

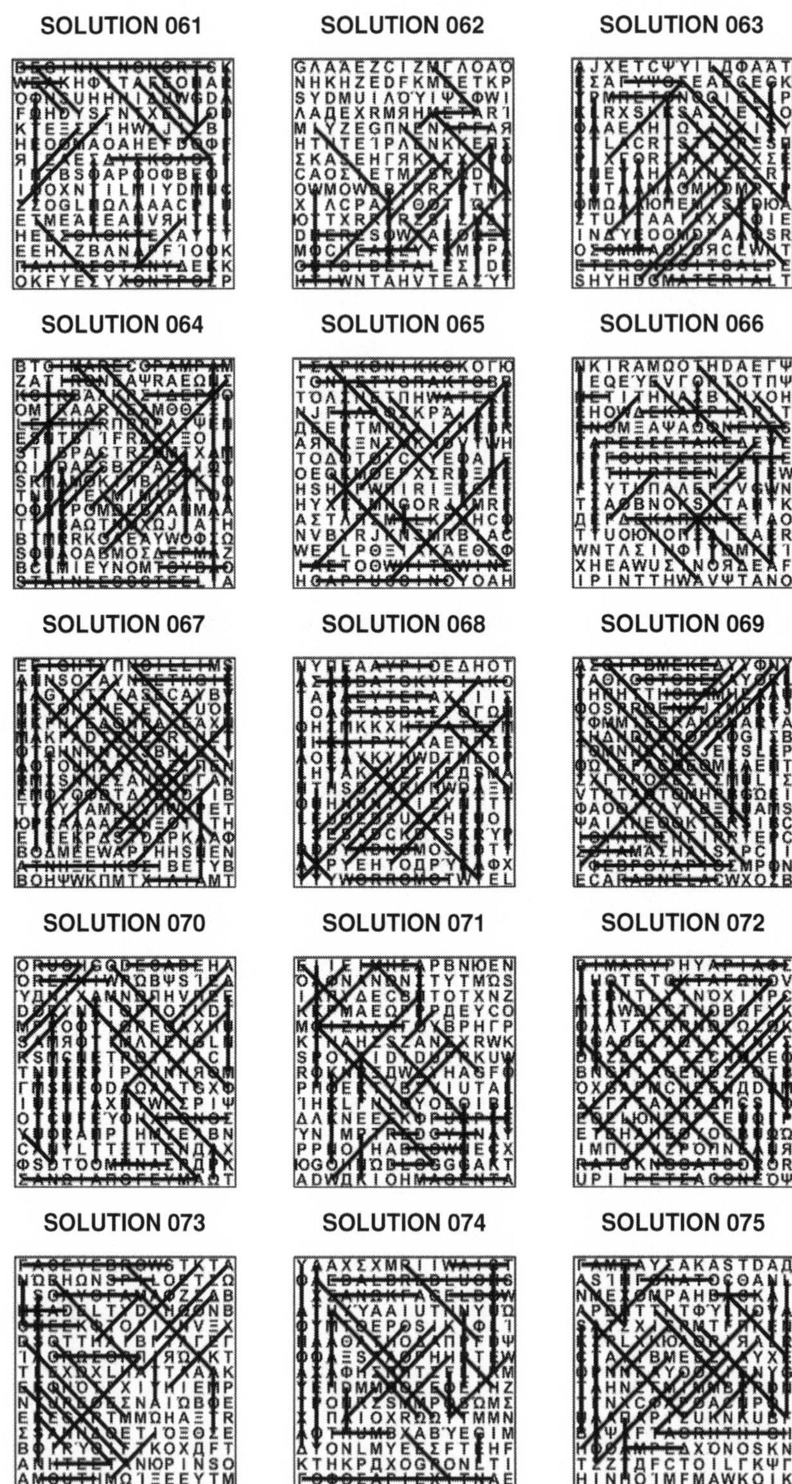
SOLUTION 061
SOLUTION 062
SOLUTION 063
SOLUTION 064
SOLUTION 065
SOLUTION 066
SOLUTION 067
SOLUTION 068
SOLUTION 069
SOLUTION 070
SOLUTION 071
SOLUTION 072
SOLUTION 073
SOLUTION 074
SOLUTION 075

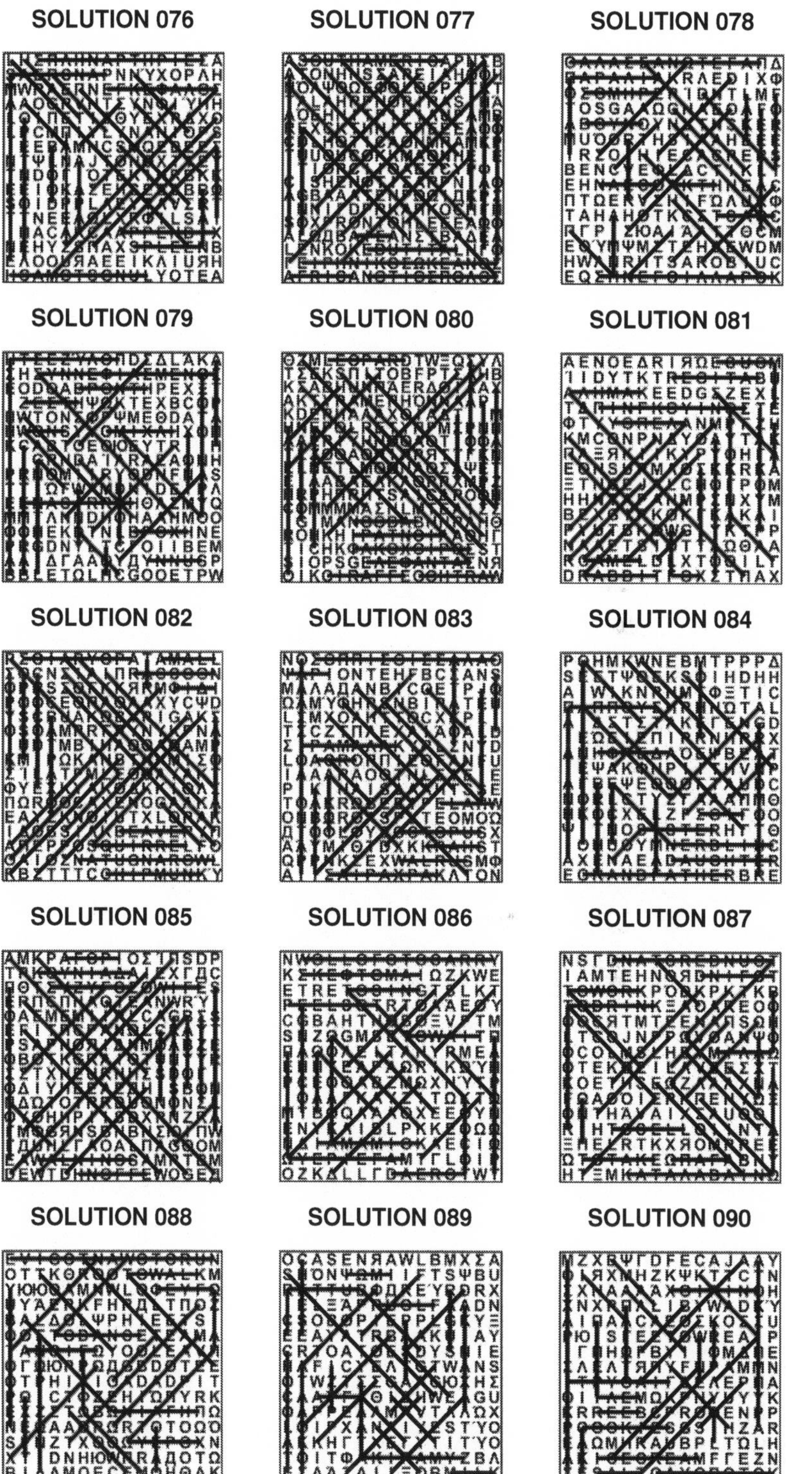
SOLUTION 076
SOLUTION 077
SOLUTION 078
SOLUTION 079
SOLUTION 080
SOLUTION 081
SOLUTION 082
SOLUTION 083
SOLUTION 084
SOLUTION 085
SOLUTION 086
SOLUTION 087
SOLUTION 088
SOLUTION 089
SOLUTION 090

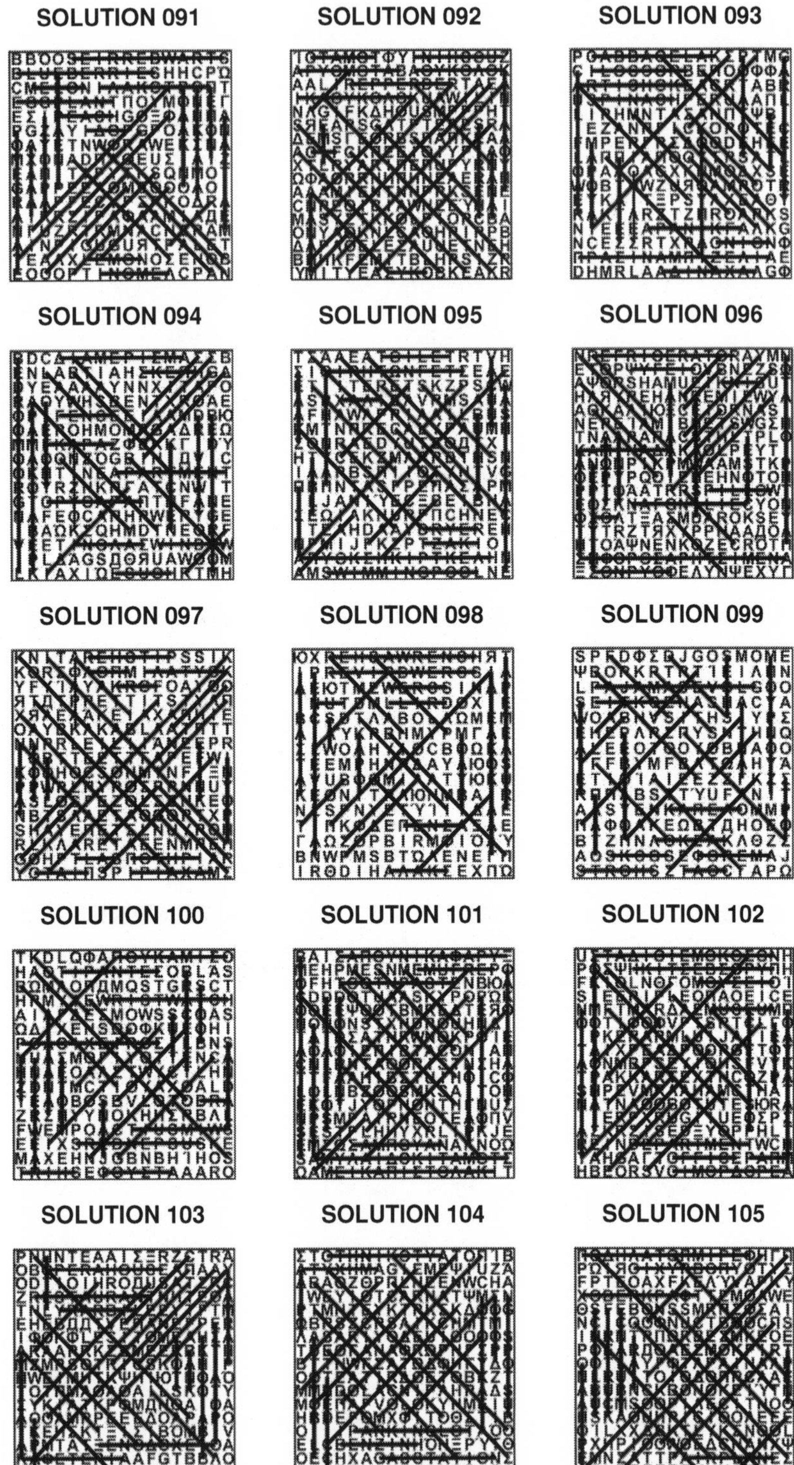
SOLUTION 091
SOLUTION 092
SOLUTION 093
SOLUTION 094
SOLUTION 095
SOLUTION 096
SOLUTION 097
SOLUTION 098
SOLUTION 099
SOLUTION 100
SOLUTION 101
SOLUTION 102
SOLUTION 103
SOLUTION 104
SOLUTION 105

SOLUTION 106

SOLUTION 107

SOLUTION 108

SOLUTION 109

SOLUTION 110

SOLUTION 111

SOLUTION 112

SOLUTION 113

SOLUTION 114

SOLUTION 115

SOLUTION 116

SOLUTION 117

SOLUTION 118

SOLUTION 119

SOLUTION 120

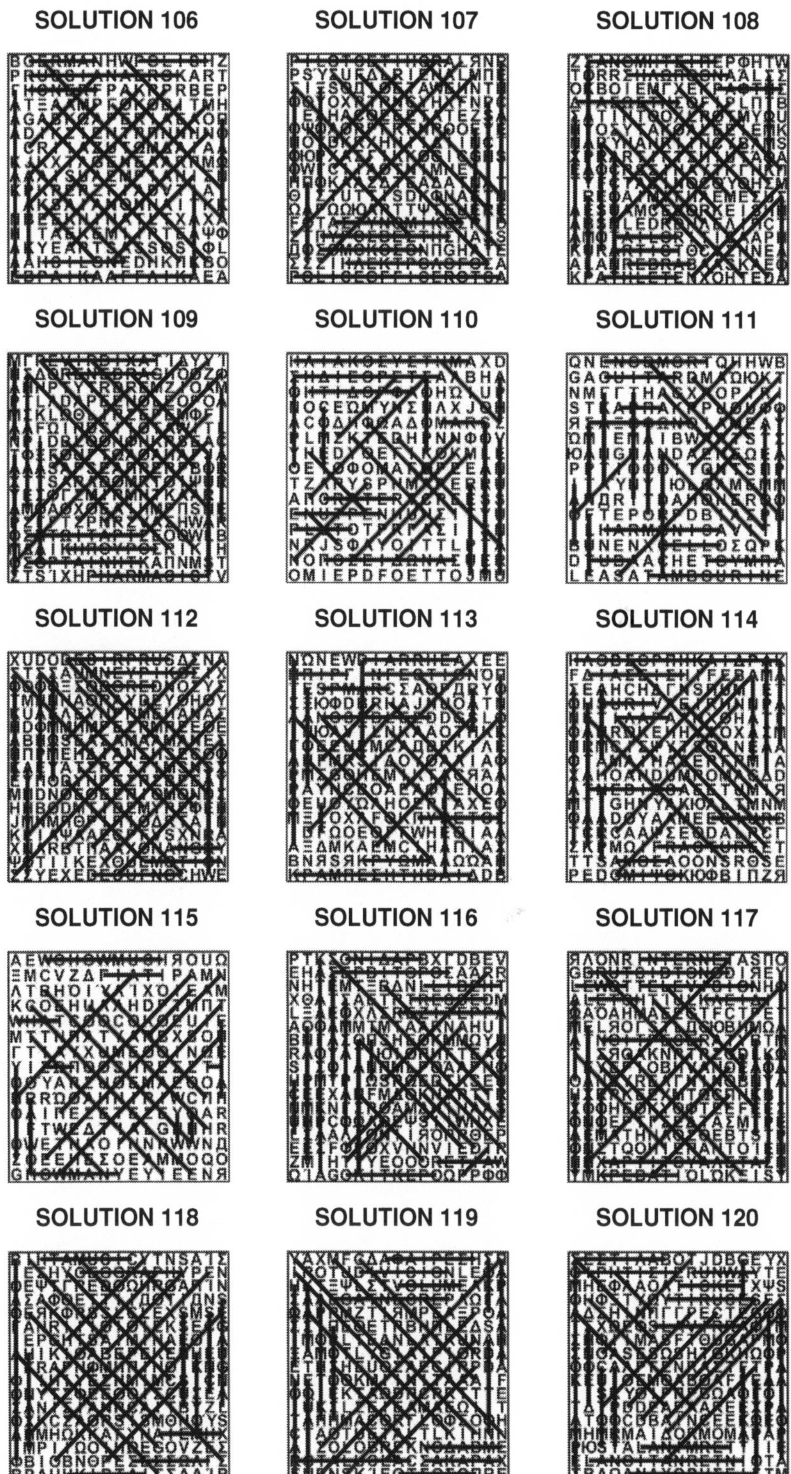

SOLUTION 121

SOLUTION 122

SOLUTION 123

SOLUTION 124

SOLUTION 125

SOLUTION 126

SOLUTION 127

SOLUTION 128

SOLUTION 129

SOLUTION 130

LEARN WITH WORD SEARCH PUZZLES
by David Solenky

Check out these other exciting books in the Language Learning series. Available on Amazon in 38 languages in regular and large print sizes.

Learn with Word Search Puzzle Books:

Albanian
Armenian
Basque
Belarusian
Brazilian Portuguese
Bulgarian
Catalan
Croatian
Czech
Danish
Dutch
Estonian
Filipino
Finnish
French
German
Greek
Hungarian
Indonesian
Irish
Italian
Japanese
Latvian
Lithuanian
Macedonian
Malay
Norwegian
Polish
Portuguese
Romanian
Russian
Serbian
Slovenian
Spanish
Swedish
Turkish
Ukrainian
Vietnamese

If you enjoyed this book, please consider leaving an HONEST review.

If you have any suggestions for future languages or books, or find any mistakes, please let us know at learnwithwordsearch@gmail.com.

Made in the USA
Middletown, DE
20 July 2020

13229837R10082